Working with Spirit

A World of Healing

By Eileen McCourt

Working with Spirit – A World of Healing

By Eileen McCourt

Working with Spirit, A World of Healing by Eileen McCourt - was first published in Great Britain in paperback during January 2016.

The moral right of Eileen McCourt is to be identified as the author of this work and has been asserted by her in accordance with the Copyright, Designs and Patents Act of 1988.

Second Edition August 2017

Contents

About the Author

Eileen McCourt is a graduate of University College Dublin, with a Master's degree in History. She is a retired professional school teacher of English and History.

A Reiki Grand Master Teacher, she teaches the following to all levels:

- Traditional Tibetan Usui Reiki

- Rahanni Celestial Healing

- Magnified Healing of the God Most High of the Universe

- Fire Spirit Reiki (Christ Consciousness and Holy Spirit)

- Archangel Reiki

- Archangel Ascended Master Reiki

- Violet Flame Reiki

- Mother Mary Reiki

- Mary Magdalene Reiki

- Unicorn Reiki

- Pegasus Reiki

- Dolphin Reiki

- Dragon Reiki

- Elemental Reiki

- Golden Eagle (Native American) Reiki

- Lemurian Crystal Reiki

- Okuna Reiki (Atlantean and Lemurian)

- Goddess of Light Reiki

- Pyramid of Goddess Isis Reiki

- Golden Rainbow Ray Reiki

- Golden Chalice Reiki
- Tera-Mai Reiki Seichem
- Psychic Surgery

Eileen has qualified in Ireland, England and Spain; in England through the Lynda Bourne School of Enlightenment; in Spain, through the Spanish Federation of Reiki with Alessandra Rossin, Bienestar, Santa Eulalia, Ibiza.

Eileen lives in Warrenpoint, County Down, Northern Ireland and has travelled extensively throughout the world.

This is Eileen's fourth book.

Her first book, '*Living the Magic: Connecting the Physical and Spiritual Worlds*', was published in December 2014.

Her second book '*This Great Awakening: The part we all play in this time of our Lives*', was published in September 2015.

Her third book, '*Spirit Calling: Are you listening?*' was published the same time as this, the fourth book, '*Working with Spirit: A World of Healing*', January 2016.

She is currently working on her first book for children, '*Young in Spirit*'.

She has also recorded several guided Meditation cd's accompanied by her brother, pianist Pat McCourt:

'*Celestial Healing*'

'*Celestial Presence*'

'*Chakra Cleansing, Energising and Balancing*'

'*Ethereal Spirit*'

'*Open the Door to Archangel Michael*'

'*Healing with Archangel Raphael*'

The list of outlets for books and cds, together with information on workshops and courses, for both practitioners and teachers, is on Eileen's website:

www.celestialhealing8.co.uk

Temple in Cambodia. Note the orbs!

ACKNOWLEDGEMENTS

I wish to express my sincere and deep appreciation to the following people, without whom this book would not have materialised:

My publishers, Don Hale OBE and Dr Steve Green for their patience and understanding;

The staff at Mourne Office Supplies, Warrenpoint, especially Bronagh, Emma and Sarah, for their friendship; for their continued support and unfailing faith in me, and for all their great work in keeping me on the road;

For my family and friends: all those here with me on the Earth Plane with whom I am linked spatially, and those who are back in Spirit, to whom I refer as 'The Ancestors', with whom I am linked lineally and whose lives have so impacted on my own;

My Reiki teachers, here in Ireland, in England and in Spain, for all they have taught me and for the help and support they continue to give me: Lynda Bourne, School of Enlightenment, West Midlands; Alessandra Rossin and Jose Luis Garcia Guerricagoitia, Bienstar, Santa Eulalia, Ibiza; Janet Kingston, Angel Times, Limerick; Mairead Murray, Dreamcatchers, Cavan; Lynn Turkington, Devata Day Spa, Portadown; Teresa Keenan, Warrenpoint.

A very special thank you to all who have bought my books and cds and attended my workshops and courses, and to those who have taken the time to write reviews for me.

Most of all, thank you, Infinite Spirit, for all the gifts and blessings which You continue to shower upon me daily, and for Your constant guidance and inspiration in the materialisation of these books.

For all of these, I am truly grateful!

Eileen McCourt

January 2016

REVIEWS

"Eileen is a very gifted healer, teacher and a wonderful writer. I have had the pleasure of learning many healing modalities from Eileen; with both her teaching and writing Eileen is able to decipher the pertinent points of the healing modality and pass it on.

I feel this book will be a huge benefit for both the beginner and well established healer, as it will give us all an understanding of the many healing modalities available out there.

Eileen's books are always easy to read and very insightful.

Keep up the great work, Eileen!"

Janet Kingston, Angel Times, Limerick

" The author has another well-written book which will be easy for all ages to understand. The reader will be enchanted and enthralled by this informative book, with insight into many non-traditional healing methods, working with the beautiful Light Beings of Unicorns and others."

Lynda Bourne, School of Enlightenment, West Midlands. (www. heavenlyguidance.co.uk)

"Once again Eileen has produced a beautiful book, this time on healing and the different beautiful modalities available to us now. Well worth reading. She has a wonderful connection with Spirit!"

Francesca Brown, the Angel Whisperer. Author of 'My Whispering Angels' and 'The Voices of Angels'.

"In 'Working With Spirit: A World of Healing', Eileen McCourt has given us a 'rarity', a must for the holistic practitioner. Now, that's a very grand claim, but in this case totally justified. 'Working With Spirit' is essentially, a thorough overview on the subtleties of energy healing. In that, Eileen has systematically de-constructed the world of energy healing and the world of the 'Reiki's', highlighting the importance of the individual perspective of the energy healing practitioners and their Guides.

Of course, the usual question arises, why so many styles, why so many alternatives? Why not just one simple form to heal the body? But, you see, to simplify this field of practice, is to minimise the importance and the power of these healing modalities and the subtle needs of the client. This is the underlying importance of Eileen's perspective. As practitioners, we are dealing with our own viewpoints, our own personal experience and, of course, our own energy. Add this then, to the multifarious and complex nature of our Guides and their energies, and we have a very intricate and staggeringly diverse range of healing energies.

As a Shamanic Practitioner and a Shamanic and Reiki Practitioner, I have found that it is an imperative to constantly build and develop my relationship with Spirit and my Guides and as I change, my Guides subtly change, thus my energy healing practice changes. Equally, it is essential to find the right fit between technique and practitioner. It is inherent in conscientious practice, therefore, that our approach is developed and researched in the most professional manner possible. Eileen McCourt has done just this and succeeded in advancing the literature on energy healing.........no mean feat.

'Working With Spirit', is purely and simply a reference book, but a hugely important one and absolutely essential for energy healing practitioners. Eileen has risen above the usual tomes on healing and has given us a broader view of the field of energy healing and with this, she has provided an invaluable resource for those on their path of holistic healing. Buy it, you'll need it!

Declan Quigley of Anam Nasca - Spiritual author and Shamanic Practitioner.

FOREWORD

There are numerous forms of healing modalities available to us right now, all of which can be very confusing for those wishing to begin their Spiritual path in channelling Celestial healing. This book is, therefore, intended for a very specific readership. Those drawn to it will either be already practising some form of Reiki healing and wishing to expand their work with additional healing modalities; or they will be interested in investigating for the first time, what the entire process is about, possibly with a view to becoming a practitioner and perhaps in time, a teacher. Alternatively, others may be drawn in their search, whether they are just beginning, or already advanced on their path to raising their own Spiritual consciousness.

We are surrounded by a vast network of higher vibrational energies, all invisible to our limited human vision, but all wishing to assist us in raising our Spiritual awareness.

A galactic tidal wave of light, a tsunami even, is being directed towards us, not to destroy us, but to help us. Masterful beings, who have graduated from earth's schoolroom, and who now have become the 'Completed Ones', are assisting mankind from the Heavenly realms; assisting mankind in every field of human endeavour; assisting mankind to raise the Spiritual consciousness of earth. These Completed Ones are willing us to reach out to them from beyond the veil, to connect with them, to bring healing to our fragmented world.

We are, literally, being offered a world of healing.

In Part One of this book, I explain the nature of Celestial Healing, and the Attunement Process, central to all healing modalities or forms of healing practice. All too often, students are unaware of what exactly an Attunement entails and of what they are actually about to undertake. Foreknowledge not only gives the student a sense of what is about to happen, but also empowers the student in an enlightening way, enabling them to get the most out of the experience.

Since 2012, new energies have evolved and are continuing to evolve, and old energies have been changed and are continuing to change, due to the earth's magnetic energy releasing blocked or negative areas. Our planet earth has had its own attunement as the gravitational and magnetic energy has been cleared and realigned by Spirit, with many new energies emerging and available to physical beings on earth as never before.

Animals are also going through radical Spiritual changes. All Spiritual beings are excited and eager to resonate with the earth's new vibration. All of us are travelling on a Spiritual journey, on a virgin path that has never before been trod.

In Part Two, I describe the various modalities of healing that are available to us now from the Celestial realms. The veils between worlds are thinning, being lifted, and we now have access to greater higher vibrational forms of energy than ever before.

All of these energies are available to all of us, with no exception. Some of them you will already be familiar with, such as Usui Reiki, Rahanni, or Angelic Reiki, and practitioner courses for these are easily available throughout the country. I feel very privileged and honoured, however, to be introducing into Ireland for the first time, from Spain and England, such Celestial healing energies as Fire Spirit Reiki (Christ Consciousness and Holy Spirit); Mother Mary Reiki; Archangel Reiki; Violet Flame Reiki; Unicorn, Dolphin, Dragon and Elemental Reiki; Golden Eagle Reiki (Native American); Goddess of Light Reiki; Golden Chalice Reiki; Okuna Reiki (Atlantean and Lemurian); Lemurian Crystal Reiki. Most of these I have mentioned require a previous attunement to traditional Usui Reiki levels One and Two. This is because these are new, powerful energies entering our earth's force field, and in order to channel them, your body needs to be already adjusted to higher forms of vibrational frequencies. Also, Reiki One opens up the body to channel for self-healing, while Reiki Two enables you to channel healing to other people. Most of these modalities can be combined with Reiki, or done on their own.

This is not a comprehensive list of healing modalities; just those energies with whom I myself work and with whom I am familiar. There are many more forms of holistic healings being practised throughout the world, and there are many more being constantly channelled from the higher dimensions, as we are now accessing the higher vibrational levels with more ease and readiness. We need practitioners of all these modalities to spread these beautiful healing energies throughout the country and make them available to everyone. There is absolutely no suggestion of competitiveness in all of these healing modalities; they are all coming from the same Divine Source, just coming via different routes; just like radio or television channels, all operating on different frequencies.

When deciding which modality to work with, follow your own intuition. You cannot go wrong in your decision. And why not? Simply because, in just the same way as you do not choose your crystal (the crystal chooses you!) so too, the particular energy chooses you. You will feel yourself being drawn to a particular modality; go with it, and feel privileged and honoured that you have, indeed, been chosen! Remember, too, that when the student is ready, the teacher will appear. Again, whomsoever you feel yourself drawn to for your teacher, trust your instincts; you are Divinely guided.

Once again, I ask that you read with an open mind and an open heart, and allow whatever parts of this book resonate most comfortably with you to bring you to a place of hope, comfort and healing. Spirit has guided you to this book, so I hope you will now allow Spirit to guide you through the various healing modalities, to bring you the help, support, and healing we are all seeking, as we continue on this, our own individual path of Spiritual evolution and the collective Spiritual evolution of all humanity.

I send you Love and Light!

Namaste!

Eileen McCourt

January 1st 2016

PART ONE: HEALING FROM THE HEAVENLY REALMS

CHAPTER 1

The Nature of Celestial Healing

The universe is a vast creation of limitless consciousness. What we, as humans can perceive with our five physical senses is only a miniscule part of all the multitudinous dimensions and vibrations that are surrounding us on all sides. Everything in the entire cosmos is energy, all in different forms, all vibrating at different frequencies. We here on planet earth are very limited in our human perception. We cannot even begin to imagine the plethora of other energies out there in the vast expanse of infinity. We as humans perceive only the physical world, but there are higher levels of mind, higher vibrations and higher dimensions of space and time stretching out into infinity that have been explored and accessed by only the 'Enlightened Ones' of humanity, those who have already progressed through the higher vibrational levels.

It is only here on planet earth that our energy takes the form of a physical body; it is only here that beings experience physicality; it is only here that souls become embodied. There are other intelligent beings that do not have physical bodies, but they do not exist on the earth plane. This is easy to accept if you believe that each person is an immortal soul, not just a physical body; but if you believe there is nothing beyond this physical existence, this earthly life-time, this physical reality perceived by the five physical senses, then you will find it difficult to accept that we are being helped by other forces outside of and beyond this physical planet earth.

We are all Spiritual beings, all evolving on our own Spiritual path. The Angels, Archangels and higher vibrational forms of energy are also continuing to evolve in order to reach the ultimate state of Completeness, which is the total merging with Divine Essence, the Oneness with 'All That Is'. We are all One. There is no separateness. We cannot evolve Spiritually on an individual basis. We can only evolve collectively. The earth plane is the most dense of all Spiritual vibrations, and so is the planet most in need of assistance and help. Hence it is, that our brothers and sisters on all other higher vibrations are willing to help us. And how does this help from the higher Spiritual dimensions manifest? This help manifests In the form of what we have come to know as 'Celestial Healing', higher vibrational energies being beamed down to our individual human frequencies.

Since 2012, the veils between dimensions have been thinning at an unprecedented and accelerated rate. Not only are old energies being altered to resonate with earth's new vibrational frequency, but more and more new energies are now penetrating our force field, tuning in to our earth vibration, all in an effort to help us raise our own Spiritual awareness and the Spiritual consciousness of all humanity.

To be able to accept and work with these new energy vibrations, we must first of all acknowledge that they exist. We need to expand our awareness, our consciousness, to go beyond our limiting five physical senses, to go beyond time and space, to realise and accept that we live in a multi-dimensional universe; that we are inter-dimensional, inter-connecting, inter-dependent beings, with a greater depth, a greater breadth than we have been conditioned in our physical body to believe.

We have to transcend the physical and merge with the Spiritual if we are to progress along our evolutionary path. Otherwise we will find ourselves stuck on the cycle of reincarnation for life-time after life-time. It is through understanding this duality of our existence, through integrating the facets of our consciousness and through accepting that the world of matter and the world of Spirit co-exist in a state of balance and harmony which enables us to move beyond our self-imposed limitations and to be able to access these other vibrational energy levels.

If we judge and perceive everything only from the perspective of our physical limitations, or from what science has led us to believe on this wavelength of planet earth, then we are denying ourselves access to the whole inter-dimensional, inter-planetary infinity of life; we are denying ourselves access to the whole vastness of creation, the whole vastness of Spirit consciousness. Science, to some extent, has limited our interpretation and understanding of life, imprisoning us within physical boundaries, taking away all the excitement, all the wonder, all the vitality, all the mystery, all the fun, reducing everything to the mundane, the ordinary, the physical. Science is denying us the merging of realities, the merging of multi-dimensional realities, vital to our Spiritual evolution.

We all know we are here for a reason. We are here on an assignment. We are here on an assignment to discover the truth. And in order to discover the truth, we have to face challenges; we have to surmount obstacles; we have to cross boundaries. And we have to transcend the boundaries that living in a physical body imposes on us, delving into the unknown, the other-worldly, searching for the path to Higher Consciousness.

This is an exciting, expanding time for Lightworkers, healers and all those who seek Spiritual development and increased Spiritual awareness. There are numerous choices available to us at this present moment, from traditional forms of holistic therapy, homeopathy, the laying on of hands, massage therapies, shamanism, prayer, to the newer modalities which have just recently been ushered into earth's plane as a direct result of the raising of earth's vibration. The Harmonic Convergence of 1987, when Lightworkers across the entire planet joined forces for the first time ever, in a joint movement of Spiritual energy; the thinning of the veil of amnesia; the 2012 cosmic alignment; the opening and re-activating of inter-dimensional portals; the mass Spiritual awakenings right across the planet, have all played their part in opening the doorways between vibrational energy levels. This has allowed higher Spiritual healing energies easier access to those of us here on earth who are willing to work with them in Love and Light for the infinite good of all humanity.

Cosmic reinforcements are waiting, ready and willing. The higher vibrational forces help the lower. If we do not accept help from those higher than us, then how can we, in turn, pass that help on to those on a lower vibration than us? We cannot!

Healing is indeed being channelled to us here on the earth's vibration, beamed in rays of Light down the 'Vibrational Corridor', along the 'Vibrational Highway'. When we use the term 'down' we do not mean down from some place up in the sky, but from a higher vibration or higher dimension. These other higher vibrational energies do not exist in a place as we understand a place to be, but are all around us on different frequencies, much like a radio station or television network. They dwell amongst us, not *'over there'* or *'up there'*. They can be called upon by any of us at any time, but in order to channel a particular energy in a healing process, an Attunement to that energy vibration is usually required.

CHAPTER 2

THE ATTUNEMENT PROCESS

THE ATTUNEMENT PROCESS is key to all forms of energy healing. Each modality has its own sacred symbol or symbols, and it is the placing of these sacred symbols by the Master Teacher into the aura, the energy field of the student or new practitioner, that activates that particular modality within the receiver.

Everyone can call in Angels, Spirit Guides, Unicorns, Dolphins, etc. to help in healing, but when we have been attuned to a certain higher vibrational frequency, then that particular form of healing can be channelled directly through our own physical body. The symbols with which you are attuned are doorways into higher forms of consciousness and stretch beyond space and time.

The attunement process is a bringing together of healing energies from the higher dimensions of reality, and the recipient is now linked into these higher energies; is now attuned to a certain frequency, and is now able to channel this energy for personal use, for friends, family, animals, plant life, situations, and all who request help and healing.

The attunement is a very beautiful experience, and must be treated with the utmost respect and reverence. It is an experience that will affect you on a deep Spiritual level, and as such will never be forgotten. Once you have been attuned to the symbols, they remain in your energetic field for the rest of your life, even if you never actually use them. The Master Teacher places them in several of your chakras, usually in your crown chakra, third eye, throat chakra, heart chakra, and both hands.

It is always important to remember that it is not the Master Teacher who actually attunes the student. The teacher is only the conduit, the tool, through which that particular healing modality energy enters into the aura of the recipient. The teacher only provides a suitable environment and a sacred atmosphere for the energy to enter. Nothing can go wrong, just as long as the teacher is coming from the heart and love. And it is the same in any healing session. Nothing can go wrong, as long as the intention of the therapist is genuine. The energy always follows the intention of the giver, but apart from that, the energy itself always knows where to go; it is not dependent on any instructions or guidance from anyone. The therapist only opens the door for the particular energy to enter and do its job. So remember! You, as the practitioner or teacher, are not the healer! You are simply opening the door for the energy to enter. Hence, as long as you remember that you yourself are not the healer, nothing can go wrong!

Each new practitioner experiences the attunement differently. This is because all our energies are individual and unique to each one of us, so when the same Divine Energy links with us, there is a unique effect on each person.

With each and every attunement, the new practitioner's body is raised to a much higher vibration of Spiritual awareness, of Spiritual consciousness, and so there is bound to be a disturbance of some sort within the system. This can manifest in light-headedness; tingling feelings like pins and needles; feeling tearful or slightly depressed. Everyone is different. There is no need to worry. This is only the physical body adjusting to the new higher level of Light energy now within it.

After an attunement, it is important to be always aware and conscious of the new higher vibration of Light energy you now carry within your physical and Spiritual body. A period of cleansing is usually advised afterwards, initially for twenty one days, in order to clear the system of toxins and denser energies. Alcohol, drugs, smoking should all be avoided, as should sugar and meat. Many new practitioners find that they go off meat completely, opting instead for a vegetarian or vegan life-style. Meat contains very dense energy. And why? Because all the animals we eat die in trauma; and by eating that meat, we are absorbing some of that trauma. The same with fish. Fish also die in trauma, gasping for breath. I myself do not eat either meat or fish; anything that has a face I just will not put into my system. I am also a vegan, and I have no difficulty finding alternatives to milk or dairy products. I do eat eggs, though, but only when I can see the hens running around freely, taking in their natural food from the earth. However, I am in no way suggesting that being a vegetarian or vegan makes me any more Spiritual than one who eats meat, fish or fowl; it is just my own personal choice and preference. I feel we are not treating animals with the respect which they deserve. They have become merely another means of making money through the lucrative food chain, in a world over-commercialised and over-devoted to materialism and materialistic pursuits.

Most new practitioners feel the flow of energy immediately after the attunement. Again, each is different. Some will feel heat coming from their hands, while others will feel coolness or cold. Again, it could be a breeze, a throbbing sensation, a tingling sensation. The client may even feel heat while the practitioner feels coolness. It is all good; the energy is flowing to where it is needed, and that is all that matters. Everyone, however, clients and practitioners alike, all feel a deep sense of peace and relaxation.

Yes! The attunement process is certainly a deeply-moving experience and affects everyone differently. When I received my first attunement with Reiki One, nothing could have prepared me for what was about to happen. I was shaken to the depths of my entire being, surrounded by the all-encompassing feeling of complete and total unconditional Love. That was my first ever Spiritual experience. And I touched my own soul that day, for the very first time in my entire life. For the very first time in my entire life, I connected with Spirit. Really, genuinely connected! And when you connect with your own soul for the very first time, you will know it! And that will remain with you forever!

That's how beautiful, empowering and overwhelming an attunement can be! It will change your life; your way of thinking; your attitudes. And once you receive an attunement, there is no going back to where you were before. You are now connected to a higher form of energy; you are now on a higher Spiritual vibration; you are now in a state of raised Spiritual consciousness, a state of raised Spiritual awareness. Something inside of you has been ignited; a light inside of you has been switched on; a mechanism inside of you has been activated. And it is all for your own higher good, and the higher good of all humanity.

Enjoy!

PART TWO: HEALING MODALITIES

CHAPTER 3

TRADITIONAL TIBETAN USUI REIKI

TRADITIONAL USUI REIKI has existed for at least 2,500 years as an oral tradition. Books were only written about it for the first time in the 1980s due to the great secrecy surrounding it, but now it is available to everyone, with Reiki practitioners and teachers in every country in the world. From a relatively unknown healing art, Reiki is now very often incorporated into treatments given by massage therapists, osteopaths, reflexologists and others to complement their standard form of practice. Everyone and anyone can learn Reiki, as it simply activates the ability inherent in us all to heal. It is one of the more widely known forms of healing affecting the flow of energy in the body, and is probably the easiest and most simple holistic healing method available to us. It is used to relieve the problems associated with chronic illness, stress, tension, emotional trauma, fear, or sadness associated with such issues as bereavement, separation, etc.

There is a life force that flows through all living things, whether human, animal, vegetable or mineral and Reiki is a technique, a means by which you can become a channel for this life force energy. It is a great tool of empowerment.

The word Reiki is made up of two Japanese words: REI, which means 'God's wisdom or the Higher Power', and KI, which means 'Life force energy'. So Reiki is actually 'Spiritually guided life force energy'.

What draws people to Reiki? Some people are drawn because they want healing; some are drawn because they want to help others; yet others are drawn because they are searching for the sense of peace, calm and fulfilment that seems to be so elusive in their everyday hectic, chaotic lives. It must always be remembered, however, that everything, absolutely everything happens in Divine Timing and in accordance with Divine Will. It must also be remembered that we do not choose Reiki; Reiki itself chooses with whom it wants to work, and if you are meant to work with Reiki, then when the time is right, you will be drawn to it.

Life force energy flows through the physical body via the chakra and meridian pathways, and around the physical body in the field of energy called the 'Aura'. This energy field responds to every thought we send out; every action that we do; every feeling we experience and when we experience negativity in any way, either consciously or unconsciously, through negative words, thoughts or actions, this energy field becomes blocked and the flow of energy is disrupted. If these blockages are not dispersed, then physical illness will manifest. Reiki is a high-vibrational, healing energy that flows through the auric field helping to release these blockages, and restoring balance and well-being to the recipient.

Reiki is beneficial not just to humans, but can also be applied to animals, plants, planets, and even situations. It transcends all religions, time and space and so It can be sent over distances, without the recipient actually having to be present. A Reiki healing is very simply performed. The practitioner channels the energy through his or her hands, over or upon the person to be healed. The energy itself knows where to go and what to do, as it is being directed by a higher intelligence, coming from Source or Spirit. The practitioner is not the healer, but is only there to facilitate the flow of energy in a conducive and sacred environment. The energy follows the intention of the practitioner, and so as long as the intention is coming from the heart and with love, the energy will flow.

During a healing session, the practitioner may temporarily experience the same symptoms as the client. Again, there is no need for worry. This is only because the therapist is working within the aura and the energetic field of the recipient, and so is feeling what the recipient feels. For example, if the receiver is suffering from a sore throat, then the therapist might well feel a sensation of tingling or dryness in the throat area, or if the recipient is suffering from a painful shoulder, then the therapist may very well experience a similar feeling in the shoulder area. This explains why and how the therapist's hands are drawn towards a certain part of the recipient's body. All the therapist has to do is acknowledge that sensation, give thanks for the message, acknowledge that the pain does not belong to him/her, and ask for it to be removed.

In order to practise Reiki, you need to be initiated by a Reiki Master, through the Spiritual empowerment of the Attunement process, based in this case, on ancient Buddhist techniques, which activates the ability to channel Reiki. Once you are attuned, the ability to channel Reiki healing energy remains with you for life, even if you never practise it. From then on, simply thinking about it, or holding your hands out in readiness to use it on yourself or on anyone else, will activate the flow of Reiki energy, which will follow the path of your intent. Every new teacher of Reiki increases the rate at which this healing modality is spread and increases the Light around the world.

Reiki brings a sense of well-being and holistic growth, unblocking and releasing inner barriers, and freeing the recipient from long-held negative emotions, grievances and deep hurt. It is a very relaxing treatment, where one can feel heat or coolness, or even a tingling sensation flowing through the body. Each of us is different and unique, and each of us has a different energy in our aura, so it is only to be expected that we will all experience different feelings, sensations and emotions during a Reiki treatment. Even if the recipient does not experience any particular feelings or sensations, it does not mean the healing is not working; the energy is still flowing.

Traditional Tibetan Usui Reiki can be traced back to Buddha, and was widely practised in Tibet over 2,000 years ago, but was lost for numerous centuries, until it was rediscovered by Doctor Mikao Usui in Japan in the early 1920's. Usui was struck down by a cholera epidemic, and nearing death, he had a Spiritual experience, which inspired him to study the Sanskrit and Sutras, the ancient teachings of his Zen Buddhist ancestors. He discovered formulas and symbols that detailed exactly how to practise and master this ancient art of hands-on healing, but felt he lacked the knowledge and wisdom to activate the power within himself. He decided to seek the answer he needed through prayer and meditation, and journeyed to the holy mountain of Kurayama. It was there, on the mountain, that he was given the answer he sought, when a bright light came towards him from the sky and entered his third eye chakra. Whilst in an altered, higher vibrational level state, he saw a vision of the same symbols he had found earlier in the Sutras. He knew he had found the keys to the ancient form of healing used by Buddha and Jesus. On his way down the mountain, he cut his toe, and when he instinctively placed his hand on it, the pain and the bleeding stopped. He was also able to heal a servant girl suffering pain from a toothache, and the Abbot in his own monastery who was suffering from severe arthritis. Usui called this gift he had received from God, Reiki, the Japanese word for Universal Life Energy.

Universal Life Energy flows through all forms of life in the entire cosmos. Illness, sickness or disease means that this energy is blocked in some way, in the mental, emotional or Spiritual bodies, manifesting in the physical. Doctor Usui developed the Usui method of healing, treating the Spirit and mind, where the problem originated, and then releasing the pain from the body. Usui died from a stroke in 1926, but not before he had initiated nineteen students to the level of Reiki Master/ Teacher. Doctor Chujiro Hayashi, a qualified physician, took over the role of Grand Master after Usui and continued the training of new Reiki Masters. His greatest advancement for Reiki was to discover the importance of whole body treatment and how the Universal Life Force would go wherever it was needed to heal, providing the whole body treatment was applied, to remove any emotional or physical blockages.

In 1940, with Japan close to war with America, Doctor Hayashi knew he would be conscripted to fight, and rather than fight, he planned to leave this incarnation, by allowing his Spirit to leave his body. Madam Takata was named as his successor and installed as the next Grand Master.

Madam Takata was Japanese, but lived in Hawaii. She herself had been healed from serious illness at Hayashi's clinic in Japan. As a result of her own healing, she decided to complete the practitioner level in Reiki training, and in 1937 she set up her own clinic in Hawaii. Hayashi felt he had found the perfect successor in Madam Takata.

Madam Takata died in 1980, having trained a further twenty-two Reiki Masters. Her work was carried on by Doctor Barbara Weber and Takata's grand-daughter, Phyllis Lei Furumoto. This partnership split up after a year, and they continued the work separately. The Reiki Alliance was formed by Phyllis Lei Furumoto, while Doctor Weber set up the American International Reiki Association. There are now several different associations throughout the world, all competing against each other and each claiming to be the only correct way of teaching Reiki.

There is, however, only one Reiki. It belongs to us all and is accessible to us all. It is a natural healing treatment for the mind, body and soul, connecting us to all living beings in a compassionate way.

There are of course occasions when Reiki will be seen not to work. This is mainly because an illness, sickness or dis-ease may be part of our own life plan, something we ourselves have chosen on our learning path through this particular life-time, and therefore cannot be removed from us.

As a Reiki practitioner, you are asked to incorporate five Spiritual principles or practices into your everyday living.

Firstly, you are asked, *just for today, to not worry*. Most doctors agree that illness is usually caused by stress. We tend to spend our mental energy trying to force the outcome that we ourselves want, instead of accepting that universal energy knows exactly what we need and want, and is manifesting that for us. We need to 'Let go and let God'; tuning into the synchronicities of events and people and accepting that we are indeed being looked after by a force greater than us, a force that has everything in order for our highest good. There is absolutely no need to worry. There is no need to fear. We are indeed being looked after by a loving Deity, an abundant universe that knows our every needs and is providing for us. By trying to force our own outcome, all we are doing is impeding the universal flow of all good things to us. Trust! Just trust!

Secondly, we are asked, *just for today, to not anger*. We need to understand that being angry is totally unproductive. Everything that happens to us happens for a reason, and every person we meet has a message for us or is offering us a learning experience. We ourselves have freely chosen and arranged all of this in our own life blue-print before we entered this incarnation. So instead of reacting to situations or people with blame or anger, we need to look for the reason behind it all, give thanks for the meaning behind it and release it with love. It is only through each individual's willingness to live in harmony with all forms of life and sending unconditional love to all, that universal peace and harmony can be established.

Thirdly, we are asked, *just for today, to honour our parents, teachers and elders.* Even if we suffer at the hands of our elders, we need to send them unconditional love. This does not mean we accept the treatment we received, but we need to grow from that experience. Sending out more of the same only increases the toxicity already out there. We are all collective energy from a single source, Divine Source, and when we show disrespect towards ourselves or any other form of life, we harm the planet and the natural harmony placed within the planet. We are all One. There is no separation. What affects one, affects all.

Fourthly, we are asked, *just for today, to live and work honestly.* Life is a balance between receiving and giving. If we are not in balance, we are not healthy. If we do not live to our full potential, we are not being honest with ourselves or with others. We have a duty to be happy, it is our natural birth right. Life is not meant to be a struggle. We are here to spread unconditional love, and to raise our own Spiritual vibration and the Spiritual consciousness of all humanity. And we cannot do that if we are not happy. And how do we get to be happy? We get to be happy by doing the things we love doing. If we are in a job that we are not happy in, then we are not in the right place, so we need to change. Going to work every day with a heavy heart or with any sense of foreboding is not conducive to our own sense of happiness and certainly of no benefit to anyone else. Living honestly simply means being happy in the life we are leading, and if we can honestly say we are happy and fulfilled, then we are connected to Spirit, we are living the life we are meant to lead. We are living and working honestly!

Fifthly, we are asked, *just for today, to give thanks for every blessing and to give gratitude to every living thing.* What we give out, we get back. If we thank the Universe for all the gifts we are constantly being given, then that sets in motion the circumstances whereby the Universe returns our gratitude to us, multiplied numerous times. We need to see ourselves as worthy of the gifts bestowed upon us, and to love ourselves enough to receive these Divine gifts. Express gratitude constantly for absolutely everything, good and bad, that comes your way. Remember, even in the bad, especially in the bad, there is a lesson for us to learn. Give thanks for that lesson!

Adherence to these five principles is inherent in Reiki. Just for today is an important consideration. The only time there is or ever can be is the present. The past is over, the future can never come, because when tomorrow arrives, or next week or next month, it is no longer the future, but is now the present. All time is merely the extended now. There is nowhere else we can ever be.

There are three degrees in Reiki Initiation. Each degree activates a particular and unique level of energy to be used for a specific purpose in healing or teaching. With each degree, the student is raised to a higher level of Spiritual consciousness, empowered to channel greater quantities of Reiki healing energy for himself and others.

The first degree, *Reiki One,* is the introductory level, taught over two days. This usually involves four attunements; an explanation of the chakras and aura; an explanation of the origin and development of Reiki; an explanation of the five ethical principles; instructions for the hand positions for self-healing and instructions for the recommended twenty one day cleansing period. The student is taught one of the three main Reiki sacred symbols. The attunement in the first degree is focused mainly on opening up the physical body, allowing the channelling of greater quantities of life force energy, and opens up the heart chakra. This first degree is the foundation of all the further degrees in Reiki and must be mastered thoroughly before the student can progress to the next degree. The Attunement in Degree One is a very empowering process and can also be very emotional, with most students reporting that it is the most memorable of all the degrees, as a deep healing experience of some kind takes place, which can affect the student in many different ways. Emotions from the past can be released, and there is also a physical response in the body. This can manifest as feelings of heat or cold, light-headedness, or even a re-emergence of old pains for a time. There is no cause for worry; this is just the body adapting itself to the new energy. After Reiki One Attunement, the student is able to practise self-healing and healing for animals, plants, objects and situations.

The second degree, *Reiki Two,* can be taken about six or eight weeks after the first degree, or even sooner, depending on how the student has been able to absorb the energy. Reiki Two provides a quantum leap in vibratory level, many times greater than the first degree. The second degree places greater emphasis on adjusting the etheric body, unlike Reiki One degree, which places more emphasis on the physical body. In addition, the throat chakra is opened, which may lead to the student experiencing a sore throat for a few days. The student is initiated further through another Attunement process, and given a further two Reiki sacred symbols with which to work. This degree also includes techniques for healing other people, for mental-emotional healing, and for sending distant healing. After this second degree, the student is now a practitioner of Reiki healing energy, and is allowed to charge a fee for their work.

The third degree, *Reiki Three*, designates the level of Mastership and Teacher of Reiki. The practitioner is now taught the Reiki Energy Master symbols and how to work with them. This attunement again amplifies the vibratory rate and activates the Master symbol so that it may be used to help others empower themselves. This symbol with which the practitioner is attuned strengthens and magnifies the energy further and is also used to initiate others into the Reiki system. In addition, the third eye chakra is greatly affected, which often leads to a heightening in the intuitive abilities of those being attuned. The final Attunement opens the crown chakra, the chakra that connects with Divine energy. With this degree, the way of practising and living in Reiki becomes more a Spiritual path. The practitioner is now a Teacher of Reiki, after being shown how to perform the Attunement process on others.

There are, however, many practitioners of Reiki who do not desire to teach Reiki, but who want to achieve the third Degree for their own Spiritual development and to get deeper into the Reiki energy work. In this case, Reiki Three degree can be taken without being shown how to attune others. With the attunement, the practitioner becomes an Inner Master, and their vibratory level is raised to facilitate the contact with their guides and their Higher Self. If they so wish later on, they can still be shown how to perform the Attunement process, so qualifying as a Teacher of Reiki.

What is a Reiki Inner Master?

A Reiki Inner Master is one who:

- Lives by the 5 Reiki principles.

- Sees everyone as Divine Light; does not judge; does not criticise.

- Sees only the good in others.

- Treats all form of life with respect.

- Practises unconditional love.

- Shows humility and compassion.

- Understands his own limitations and ability.

- Feels no self-importance.

- Shows patience, tolerance and understanding of others.

- Refrains from personal abuse, such as drugs, alcohol, etc.

- Is true to himself.

- Honours his I AM PRESENCE, remembering who he really is.

- Continues to seek knowledge in different Spiritual areas.

- Continues to practise Reiki on himself and on others.

- Shows integrity, commitment and insight.

Reiki is a Spiritual experience of transmission of love that fills you, satisfies your doubt and nourishes your soul. It makes you feel part of the energetic frequency of the pure love which you are now channelling. Once you have been initiated through the Attunement process, the energy will continue to flow through you, assisting you to maintain good health and live a joyful, relaxed life. The Reiki energy is a sacred energy and must be treated at all times with the utmost respect. It is a beautiful healing gift to the world, relieving suffering, bringing inner peace and balance, and when combined with living life in accordance with the five Spiritual Reiki principles, guarantees a healthy, fulfilling, balanced and harmonious existence, as you walk the path of healing love.

CHAPTER 4

TERA-MAI REIKI SEICHEM

TERA-MAI REIKI SEICHEM is of the same lineage as Traditional Usui Reiki. It uses the same symbols, but was expanded as a form of healing by Kathleen Milner, renowned world psychic and healer, channelling through Buddha. Tera-Mai Reiki is usually taught alongside Usui Reiki, and works to repair the aura as well as the physical body, helping to remove blockages.

Tera-Mai Reiki Seichem combines all four elemental forces: Fire, Water, Air and Earth.

Fire Energy (Sakara) works on the aura, the electromagnetic field surrounding the physical body. One of the main properties of Fire is transmutation, so Sakara, in healing, burns through and dissolves blockages in the physical, mental, emotional and Spiritual bodies.

Science as yet has not come up with an explanation of the phenomenon that we call Fire. And why not? Why has science, that claims to have mostly all the answers, still not been able to give us a rational explanation of what we take so much for granted in our every day lives?

The answer lies in the fact that science sees only through the five physical senses that we operate through on this third dimensional vibration of earth. Fire comes from the fourth vibrational dimension; lightning from the fifth. Science fails to recognise other-worldly vibrational dimensions, hence its failure to explain other-dimensional energies; it is looking in the wrong place! Fire at the healing level is the vessel which holds Angelic Light, which is the healing aspect of

Air, surrounding the body with protective light. Clients often feel charges of electricity through their body during a healing session.

Water Energy (Sophiel) reaches deep into the core within the emotional body for deep emotional healing, opening the heart to receive love and to feel compassion.

Air energy (Angelic Light) is a two-fold ray working with both the Air element and the Angelic Realm, enabling the healing facilitator to work effectively with Angels.

Earth energy is referred to by the Masters as 'Tera-Mai', meaning 'my earth'. Earth energy is a grounding energy, bringing Spiritual energy to earth, literally, and without it, nothing else will happen on the physical plane. Usui Reiki, which works mostly with earth energy, is, therefore, fundamental to all of the other elemental healing rays.

In Japan, over one hundred years ago, Reiki practitioners referred to themselves as '*Masters'*, because they incorporated all four elemental energies into their healing practice, the same four elemental energies that comprise our physical human bodies.

As well as the Reiki Attunements, Tera-Mai Reiki Seichem usually also incorporates initiation into the Violet Flame; the Order of Melchizedek; and an explanation of the technique of Psychic Surgery.

CHAPTER 5

ARCHANGEL REIKI

ARCHANGEL REIKI is a beautiful merging of the energies of the seven Archangels used in this healing, together with the Spiritual energies of the recipient and the therapist.

All forms of life continue to evolve Spiritually. So too, the Angels and Archangels are also on their Ascension path, earning their brownie points and gaining higher, Spiritual vibrational levels, according to how well they do their job with us.

Angels are beings of pure Light, and are now with us at this time in greater numbers than ever before, to help in this massive shift in the earth consciousness and the Spiritual evolution of all humanity. 2012 ushered in a new influx of higher vibrational energies, and Angels are now flocking to all corners of the earth. They surround us with loving acceptance and non-judgement, seeing us all as the bright shining Light, that spark of Divine Essence that each of us truly is.

Everything is now changing, and the universe is re-arranging itself to adapt to that change. When we connect with the Angels, we expand and grow in our own Spiritual development, and we become closer to the realisation that we are wonderful beings, spreading Love and Light around our beloved planet earth.

Angels have been known to us for centuries, and have featured in all religious traditions. Medieval artists such as Michelangelo and Leonardo da Vinci have put a shape and form to them for us in their paintings. There have been great surges of Angels flocking to earth throughout history, and we are now experiencing another such surge, as Angelic beings flock to our earthly dimension to assist us in raising our Spiritual consciousness.

Angels, being very high Spiritual beings and pure Light, operate on a much faster, much higher vibration than we humans, and unlike humans, they have never incarnated on this earth plane, with the exception of the two Archangels, both of whose names each end with the letters 'on': Archangel Metatron, who was incarnated as the wise man *Enoch,* and Archangel Sandalphon who was the prophet *Elijah.*

Angels are Divine messengers, here to serve humanity and to guide and protect us on our Spiritual path. They always radiate love, compassion and peace. Because their vibration is so pure and high, they are invisible to us, except for those amongst us - mystics, visionaries and mediums, who are able to raise their own vibration high enough to facilitate a meeting. Otherwise, we can experience them through a sensing, a knowing, a feeling, that they are all around us; a soft, loving, peaceful feeling that completely cocoons us in a bath of unconditional love.

What the Angels cannot do, however, is intervene in our lives without our specific request for them to do so. We have to invite them into our lives, as we all have free will, and that free will cannot be compromised. Also, they will never interfere with us learning the lessons we have come here to learn. They are here to help us learn those lessons; they will not make our decisions; nor will they remove those lessons for us. They will remind us of the task we have taken on, as they hold the blue-print of our life's plan, our soul's mission and purpose here on earth.

It is far beyond our limited human understanding as to all that the Angels do, but there are Angels for every conceivable eventuality, from healing and transmutation; mercy; forgiveness; compassion; miracles; nature; children; protection; pardon; perseverance; supreme knowledge and wisdom; even Angels who will fix electrical or plumbing faults! The list is endless! And they are always on call 24/7! How's that for service?

There is also a hierarchy within the Angelic Realms. The higher vibrational energy levels of Angels are the *Dominions,* the *Seraphim* and *Cherubim,* and these are occupied with higher vibrational levels of life form, many of these civilizations existing millions of light years ahead of us, but still Spiritually evolving. It is the Guardian Angels, Angels and Archangels who are nearest to us here on the earth's vibrational plane, and who are responsible for raising the Spiritual consciousness of humanity. The vibration of the earth has been raised with the recent re-alignment of our planetary system, and our present earth's vibration now resonates more closely with that of the Angelic Kingdom, enabling humanity to merge and work with Angelic beings as never before. Hence it is that Angelic and Archangel Reiki have now become available to us.

In Archangel Reiki, the Angel for the attunement is the '*Angel of Presence'.* This Angel has been with you all your life, a bridge of connection with Divine Source, working with your Guardian Angel. This Angel sees all the good inside you; your inner beauty; and knows where you are in your Spiritual development; what you are learning, and your level of consciousness. This Angel knows your thoughts, your emotions, and sees the beauty of your Light, with no judgement, only unconditional Love and acceptance. You are indeed greatly loved!

Like all forms of Angelic Reiki, Archangel Reiki is a merging of the Archangel energies with the client and the practitioner. As the practitioner, your hands remain on the client's shoulders; you visualise yourself as one with the Archangel, - eyes to eyes, face to face, hands to hands, until you can see yourself through your Angel's eyes. You are part of the Angel.

This attunement with the Archangels enables you to channel this energy for yourself, your friends, or whoever asks you.

There are seven Archangels with whose energy you are attuned, with a different symbol for each Archangel. Each of these seven Archangels has different attributes:

- **Archangel Michael** brings strength and protection, and helps you to destroy old habits which no longer serve you;

- **Archangel Raphael** brings healing, abundance, wholeness, unity and Divine connection;

- **Archangel Gabriel** brings guidance, vision, inspiration, communication skills and teaches you to live by your heart;

- **Archangel Uriel** brings peace and tranquillity, prosperity, and helps you to change your energy in order to attract what you need;

- **Archangel Anael** helps with all kinds of relationships and teaches you to love yourself;

- **Archangel Jophiel** brings Spiritual knowledge, wisdom, connection with Source and your Guardian Angel;

- **Archangel Metatron** brings knowledge of the higher dimensions, increases your Light energy levels, energises your chakras, and transmutes negativity.

You must be very aware and very conscious after your Attunement, of the purity of the energy with which you are now attuned, and which you now carry in your force field and aura.

Be open to whatever happens in your life, knowing that these mighty Archangels are with you every step of the way, surrounding you in wings of loving Light.

CHAPTER 6

REIKI FIRE SPIRIT (CHRIST CONSCIOUSNESS AND HOLY SPIRIT)

This healing energy, **Reiki Fire Spirit,** is from the highest vibration, coming from The Holy Spirit, through The Christ Consciousness, opening us and calling us to do everything in the name of Jesus Christ, bringing unconditional Love and Light to whoever desires.

For the Attunement, we have to open our hearts to Jesus and accept Him as our Lord and Saviour, and ask that the Flame of the Holy Spirit stays in our hearts, and through this, we can manifest the wonderful power of the Love of Jesus.

As new practitioners, it is not just an attunement that we are receiving. We are receiving Spiritual Baptism with the Fire of The Holy Spirit that lies in our hearts, fulfilling our lives, healing our physical, emotional, mental and Spiritual body and bringing us to a higher level of Spiritual evolution.

This Reiki Fire Spirit makes us Light Warriors, giving us the tools to face the issues that present themselves to us daily. As Light Warriors, we will receive the armour of Holy Spirit, and as brothers and sisters, we get stronger in the Lord Jesus, with His strength and power.

This system strengthens us against evil as we Spiritually fight against lower energies. The armour of Jesus Christ enables us to resist these lower energies and survive strongly.

We stand firmly, shoulder to shoulder with the truth, with justice and with Angelic peace. We take the helmet of Salvation and the sword of The Holy Spirit, as we get attuned with the power of the healing of

Jesus Christ through His unconditional Love, opening and strengthening our channel for healing.

There are three sacred symbols for use in this healing modality, all connected with the Heart of Jesus and with Holy Spirit.

The first symbol, the '*Heart of Jesus*', is used for attunements, and, coming on the vibration of the Holy Spirit, calls on the Spirit of God to descend and live in our hearts.

The second symbol incorporates the '*Cross of Jesus*' and the Infinity sign and is for healing in presence or distance, invoking the power, Light and Love of Jesus Christ.

The third symbol also incorporates the '*Cross of Jesus*' and is for protection, to be used to end the Reiki session or when you start your day.

A truly amazing, wonderful and magnificent healing energy!

CHAPTER 7

MOTHER MARY REIKI

MOTHER MARY REIKI is one of the most powerful systems of healing energy which has emerged after the introduction of traditional Usui Reiki. This energy healing was given to Ethel Lombardi in America in 1983. Ethel Lombardi is an international healer and teacher, attuned by Hawayo Takata, the third traditional Usui Reiki Grand Master, after Doctor Usui himself and Doctor Hayashi.

Mother Mary Reiki includes three additional symbols to the traditional Usui Reiki symbols. These new symbols are very strong and powerful, allowing all memories of our body to be regenerated. The theory of this Reiki is based on the fact that each cell in our body has a memory. It is now generally accepted that everything is recorded in memory cells. These memories hold emotional or psychic experiences that might block the natural flow of the energy.

In Mother Mary Reiki, the therapist channels the energy of the Divine Mother in a very loving way. This Mother Mary energy is used especially to treat conflict in families and can be used for trauma or unforgiveness; these lower energies will not allow the person to grow, causing emotional imbalance.

Mother Mary energy is the essence of the feminine, to rebalance the masculine energy in the world today. Reiki Mother Mary is here to bring perfect balance, with the wonderful qualities of Love, Compassion and Giving.

Mother Mary Reiki can be combined with all other therapies or the symbols can be used on their own. All will benefit from the blessing and gentle healing of Divine Mother.

This Holy Mother Mary Reiki gives connection to Divine Vibration, with the energy being channelled in a very gentle way. The therapist can either touch or not touch the recipient. The energy heals deeply, physically and emotionally.

Mother Mary healing energy goes deep into the soul and helps to remove all blockages, repeated destructive patterns, trauma and pain, as the symbols combine perfectly with the traditional Usui Reiki symbols, attending to the particular needs of the recipient, at the loving hands of Mother Mary.

The energy is gentle, loving and soft. It can never be hurtful, and never any more than the person can take. Very often just one session is enough. Additional sessions can be taken to go deeper.

Mother Mary heals with universal love and compassion, Her feminine energy allowing the release of trauma and blockages, like a beautiful adventure that transforms the soul.

Coming from the Heart of Mother Mary, this energy brings us back to the feminine, in unconditional love and compassion. We see our own lives through intuition and feeling and we give back to our emotional feelings in a healthy way.

Mother Mary energy is also the energy of Quan Yin, who is the Chinese version of Mother Mary.

There are three symbols in Mother Mary Reiki. They can be used in conjunction with traditional Reiki or separately. The therapist's hands are placed on each of the client's chakras in just the same way as traditional Reiki.

The first symbol, the '*Crown Chakra Symbol*', is drawn down over the body of the recipient, starting and ending with the crown chakra, and spreading blue energy all through the body. This activates the healing of Mother Mary for both the therapist and recipient and connects with Mother Mary.

The second symbol, the '*Power Symbol*', carries the Mother Mary healing vibration and is used to remove blockages.

The third symbol, the '*Absent Symbol*', is used for distance healing and is visualised or drawn on the hands of the sender.

A truly beautiful energy with which to work!

CHAPTER 8

VIOLET FLAME REIKI

VIOLET FLAME REIKI has been channelled from the Ascended Masters Saint Germain and Quan Yin. The Violet Flame is used to remove and transmute negative energy, replacing it with positive, pure Violet Flame Energy, violet being a high vibrational colour of healing and transmutation.

The Ascended Masters are our brothers and sisters in Spirit who have graduated from earth's school ahead of us; have balanced their karma; have fulfilled their unique mission and have ascended back to Divine Source in the Spiritual ritual known as '*Ascension*'. These Masters are now a vast brotherhood of Spiritual and Celestial beings; beings of Light; beings who serve humanity; beings who work with mankind for the betterment of life on earth. They have emerged from all races and nationalities, from all religions and all walks of life. Many have not re-incarnated for numerous centuries, and are not even recorded in human history. Many, however, are well known to us, as they have walked amongst us for life-time after life-time here on this earth plane. Those best known to us include Jesus Christ, Moses, Buddha, Maitreya, Lord Melchizedek, Mother Mary, Saint Francis, Lady Quan Yin, Lady Portia, El Morya. No longer confined to a mortal frame or limited by earth dimension, these Ascended Masters are now totally devoted to sharing Divine Light and universal and Divine truth with us who are still here on the earth plane, helping us to advance our Spiritual evolution.

Ascended Master, Saint Germain, whose name derives from the Latin 'Sanctus Germanus', meaning 'Holy Brother', is often referred to as 'The Count' because of his aristocratic lineage in the life-time into which he was born in 1561. Later, in the 1700s, he was known as the 'Wonder Man of Europe'. Accomplished in many languages, an excellent horseman, a skilled swordsman, a master violinist, he helped the poor and worked for peace, befriending many of the European heads of State.

In life-times previous to these he was embodied as a ruler, priest, prophet, discoverer and scientist, amongst others.

Over 50,000 years ago, Saint Germain was the ruler of a golden-age civilisation in a rich fertile country where the Sahara Desert is now located. As King-Emperor, he was keeper of the ancient wisdom and knowledge for his people.

Saint Germain was the High Priest of the Violet Flame Temple in Atlantis 13,000 years ago and in that role, he sustained, by his invocations and his high- vibrational causal body, a pillar of fire, a Violet Flame which provided freedom to people from every binding condition of body, mind and soul. The causal body is the highest of the vibrational bodies surrounding our physical body, and its content is the accumulation by slow and gradual process, of the good in each life.

This Violet Flame was removed from earth's vibration after the people of Atlantis abused their power and misused the Violet Flame energy for their own gains. Atlantis was a highly evolved civilisation which existed over 13,000 years ago. The Ascended Masters have been waiting until the time is right in order to return the Violet Flame to the earth plane. The current process of change in human consciousness and the raising of human Spiritual awareness since the 1987 Harmonic Convergence, has resulted in the Violet Flame being restored to humanity. The 1987 Harmonic Convergence was a time when Light Workers around the world came together, for the first time ever, in a universal joining of energies to assist in raising the vibration of the earth. Then the Violet Flame was slowly reintroduced back to the earth for the use of Lightworkers around the world.

In the eleventh century A.D., Saint Germain was embodied as the prophet 'Samuel', and led his people, the Israelites, in a great Spiritual revival in the face of their struggles against the Philistines.

Later, he became embodied as Saint Joseph, the father of Jesus and husband of Mary. He is said to have been a carpenter, though teaching Jesus much more than carpentry. He is thought to have been the one who taught Jesus the art of alchemy, illustrated by Jesus changing the water into wine at the wedding feast at Cana. Alchemy was practised by the ancients as an art or ability to change base metals into gold, as well as a universal cure for disease, - a panacea, and a means to indefinitely prolong life,- an elixir of life.

In the late third century, Saint Germain was embodied as Saint

Alban, the first martyr of Britain. Alban lived in England during the persecution of Christians under the Roman Emperor, Diocletian. He was a pagan who had served in the Roman army and settled in the town of Verulamium, later renamed Saint Albans. Alban hid a fugitive Christian priest named Amphibalus, who converted him. When Alban helped the priest to escape from the town, he was scourged and condemned to death.

In the fifth century, Saint Germain was embodied as Merlin, known as the magician who lived at the Court of King Arthur, acting as alchemist, prophet and councillor, and leading King Arthur through twelve battles in order to unite the Kingdom of Britain. As Merlin, Saint Germain was a wise sage, studying the stars and prophesising future events.

In more recent centuries, Saint Germain was Roger Bacon, born in 1220; philosopher, Franciscan Monk, educational reformer, and most of all, experimental scientist. As Roger Bacon, he was renowned for his investigations into alchemy, optics, mathematics, astrology and languages. Today, Roger Bacon is regarded as the prophet and the instigator of modern technology.

In 1451, Saint Germain became embodied as Christopher Columbus, discoverer of America. Over 200 years before Columbus set sail, Roger Bacon himself had prepared the way for Columbus' voyage of exploration to the New World as he taught that one could reach India by sailing westward. Even though this was not exactly correct, as America lay in between, Bacon's teachings nevertheless became the inspiration for Columbus' explorations. Columbus himself always believed that he himself had been Divinely selected for his mission. As Christopher Columbus, Saint Germain had several recollections of his previous life in the temple on Atlantis, and recorded how he felt himself drawn towards the submerged location of that temple, which went under water with the flooding of Atlantis.

Embodied yet again, as Francis Bacon this time, born in 1561, Saint Germain was a philosopher, writer, statesman, gathering around him a group of writers, the greatest of the Elizabethan Age. It is strongly now believed by many that it was Francis Bacon who actually wrote Shakespeare's plays. Some scholars of the Elizabethan Age even maintain that he was the son of Queen Elizabeth, the product of her love affair with her famous courtier Lord Leicester, but denied by her because she wished to keep her reputation of '*Virgin Queen*' intact.

Even after his Ascension, Saint Germain was granted permission to return to the earth plane in a physical body, to continue his work in bringing truth, and therefore freedom, to humanity. He became the 'Wonder Man of Europe' as the Count of Saint Germain; scholar, poet, musician, linguist, artist, diplomat, dazzling his way around the courts of eighteenth and early nineteenth century Europe. The French King, Louis XV, granted him a laboratory and residence at the royal Castle of Chambord, where he conducted his alchemical experiments and demonstrations and where, amongst other astonishing feats, he removed flaws in diamonds and other precious stones. He attempted to stem the flow of blood during the French Revolution, and foretold the execution of King Louis XV and Queen Marie Antoinette.

Saint Germain is known in the heavenly realms as the master alchemist. He teaches the science of alchemy in his book '*Saint Germain On Alchemy*'. He uses the amethyst, the stone of the Aquarian age and the Violet Flame.

Alchemy is the 'all-chemistry of God', the science that enables us to access the universal Light. For Saint Germain, the highest alchemy is the science of self-transmutation, which leads us into total Christ Consciousness.

Saint Germain's successive embodiments testify to the fact that we all are of a particular soul type; an on-going soul type, reincarnating life-time after life-time to complete and fulfill our mission as that soul type. Saint Germain obviously chose the path of bringing enlightenment and truth to mankind, as evidenced in his continued collective life-times as exploring new truths through science, experiments, writing, alchemy, philosophy, prophecy, new devices, all in pursuit of humanity acquiring God-realisation and Spiritual advancement.

Ascended Master Lady Quan Yin helps Saint Germain spread the word about the Violet Flame. She is the eyes and ears on the ground, coordinating the Lightworkers here on earth and Saint Germain, with heavenly intervention from above.

Quan Yin is the Chinese version of Mother Mary, and is especially helpful with children and families. Wherever you go in Far Eastern countries, you will see statues of Quan Yin guarding mountains, towns, villages, and entrances to harbours and homes. She is responsible for the honesty and integrity among the Chinese, a task of mammoth proportions, considering the dense vibration in which China now operates.

The name Quan Yin is a shortened version of the name that means '*One Who Sees and Hears the Cry from the Human World*'. Quan Yin was originally a man when in an earth body, then through time reached Enlightenment and was given the opportunity to remain in the higher realms as an Ascended Master. Quan Yin chose to remain on the earth plane as a Spiritual being to help mankind prepare for 2012 and Ascension, and will remain in that role until all sentient beings on earth have attained Ascension.

Quan Yin is known as the Goddess of Mercy, Compassion and Forgiveness. Her service to mankind is mercy and healing and She, with Mother Mary and Isis, are a Trinity of Goddesses who are in charge of directing the healing activity to mankind here on the earth plane. Quan Yin is patroness of children and of birth, and can be called upon for assistance to overcome all types of discord.

Saint Germain, Archangel Zadkiel and Ascended Master Quan Yin all work with the Violet Flame, Saint Germain being 'Lord of the Seventh Ray'.

The Seventh Ray is known as the Violet Ray. Spiritual Light manifests in seven rays, (seven colours of the rainbow). Each ray has a specific colour, frequency and quality of God's Consciousness. The Violet Ray is a tool to help us to accelerate our Spiritual growth. The Violet Flame works on all levels, physical, mental, emotional and Spiritual, but its main purpose is to remove negative energy from the physical body. It is used mostly on the earth's plane, as it is here on earth where the most negative energy is felt. When you feel the need to send healing to our planet, then the Violet Flame is the best energy to use, with its high frequency being able to penetrate denser and heavier energy, lower energies shrinking in fear of its intense power.

Quan Yin was Chohan or Lord of the Seventh Ray but in the latter part of the eighteenth century Saint Germain took over that office and is now directing the consciousness of mankind for this next two thousand year period. Together with his twin Flame, Ascended Master Lady Portia, he is the Hierarch of the Aquarian Age.

The Age of Aquarius is an era of peace, freedom and enlightenment, and it is for this Age of Aquarius that Saint Germain and Quan Yin have been preparing us over the last number of years. Saint Germain and Quan Yin are two of the Ascended Masters who have been encouraging interest amongst us in Spiritual healing, and encouraging also the idea of the internet to make all downloading of information accessible to everyone. The full strength of the Violet Flame could not be brought to Earth all at one time, so has been attuned in three stages, with the help of Reiki Masters working throughout the world. In 1984 the Violet Flame's gentler energy was reintroduced to healers on earth, then the more powerful Silver Violet Flame, and then most recently, the intense Golden Violet Flame.

The Violet Flame is also connected with Unicorns. Unicorns surround themselves with the Violet Flame energy for protection when working with healers on our earth vibrational level. The Violet Flame energy transmutes any negative energy which might try to attach itself to the Unicorn's pure energy. Unicorns work within the Angelic realms and the colour gold, but when working with their human healer, they use the Violet Flame.

After your Attunement, the Violet Flame, when invoked, descends on a beam of Spiritual energy above your crown chakra. This will then travel down your central column (spine) and connect with your kundalini energy at the base of your spine. The Violet Flame will use pulses of energy to increase the Violet Flame frequency so you can remove negativity from yourself or heal others. The Violet Flame's special quality is that it transmutes negative emotional energy which helps many people who suffer from depression or low self-esteem. The Violet Flame is very much earth energy, and helps the physical body to remove negative toxins, which in turn helps the mind, soul and well-being of the individual. Mainly the Violet Flame works with people rather than animals, as rarely do animals suffer from anxiety caused by emotional logic. The Violet Flame works by pulsing wave energy to move the denser negative energy, then the Flame will lift and convert this heavier, negative energy into silver light energy. The Violet Flame raises your level of Spiritual consciousness and links you to higher Spiritual dimensions.

Archangel Zadkiel's name means '*Righteousness of God*'. He works on the Silver Violet Ray helping Saint Germain. He is the Archangel of mercy and benevolence, probably because he stopped Abraham from sacrificing his son, Isaac, as an offering to God. Archangel Zadkiel will help you with new ideas and concepts by releasing fear and karmic blockages. He works with Archangel Michael when removing negative etheric cords which are preventing you fulfilling your life's purpose. Invariably he will show himself as a column of violet light with silver flashes.

The Violet Flame can be used to heal our planet by sending it to any place where there is conflict or trauma. The earth has concentrated vortex-energy centres and ley lines, similar to our chakras and meridians, and those attuned to Violet Flame Reiki can send the Violet Flame to these areas. The heart centre of the earth is in Glastonbury, Southern England, and even in medieval times, people understood the importance and Spiritual significance of that particular place. The Violet Flame can also be sent right around the world, regardless of where there is, or is not conflict, and through the earth's underworld, to help with releasing negative souls, in the hope that they will follow the beam of energy and arrive back in the Light where they will be healed. Never doubt that your intent has been carried through. Always trust and know that your intent is very powerful, as it is your intent which sends out the vibration of energy which activates the energy which you invoked. That is the power you have! The power to heal the world! The power to heal Mother Earth, all in her and all on her!

The purpose of your soul's evolution on earth is to grow in self-mastery, balance your karma and fulfill your mission on earth so that you can return to the Spiritual dimension, requiring no further physical embodiments. The use of the Violet Flame can help you reach that goal more quickly.

The symbols used in Violet Flame Reiki are numerous and you will use only those to which you feel particularly drawn. Different symbols apply to the physical body, the mental body, the emotional body and the soul.

After your Attunement, and as a Violet Flame Reiki practitioner, you will be able to help people who are Spiritually closed down, to clear their stress on the earth level and to once again enjoy Spiritual experiences. Use the power of the Violet Flame to bring happiness to yourself and others by removing and transmuting negativity. Use your powerful thoughts to bring in help and guidance wherever you feel it is needed. With the help of the Violet Flame, you will have the magic to transform our beloved Mother Earth and all that live on her.

Never underestimate the powerful good you can do with the help of the Violet Flame!

CHAPTER 9

ANGELIC REIKI

ANGELIC REIKI, described as *"The Healing for our Time"* by non other than Archangel Metatron, is a unique gift to humanity. Channelled by Kevin and Christine Core, Angelic Reiki brings to the earth plane the high vibrational energies of the Angelic Kingdom of Light. Kevin has now passed back to Spirit, but his work is carried on by Christine. Kevin himself described Angelic Reiki as *"the absolute joy of working hand in hand with The Angelic Kingdom of Light to bring one of the highest forms of healing to individuals, groups and the planet."*

Divine Plan is, and continues to unfold on earth. It is difficult for us, with our very limited human vision, to see or to understand what a hugely significant time this is right now for all of humanity here on planet earth and for the entire cosmos.

Why is Angelic Reiki here now?

Angelic Reiki is here now because we have finally begun the long process of returning to our Divine Connectedness. For the last two thousand years and more, mankind has been slipping further and further away from Divine Connection, into the depths of gross materialism. Our connection to Divine Source, our connection to our Divine inherent Essence, became shrouded through the mists of time, leaving us adrift in a vast wilderness. We became Spiritual exiles who had lost all communication with our natural home.

All existence is based on vibration, and the vibration in which earth exists has been raised with the recent re-alignment of the planetary system, hence allowing into the earth plane, higher Celestial vibrations.

Great shifts have been taking place in the earth's energy field, in human consciousness and in our ability to re-connect with the Spiritual and Celestial Kingdoms. Several great time-cycles in our solar system have come to an end; we are mutating and evolving into beings of greater Light bodies; awakening to our inherent awareness that we are Divine Essence, immortal, infinite; destined now to merge with Angelic beings to receive help, comfort and healing, as we leave behind our disconnectedness and follow the path towards a new, glorious Age. Our human consciousness and the consciousness of the Angelic Kingdom are now able to merge and work together for the good of all.

The Angelic Kingdom brings us untold gifts and blessings, far beyond our human comprehension. Angelic Reiki offers humanity a deep and intimate relationship with the Angelic Kingdom of Light, opening the door-way for us to merge with them, to work with them to bring a new dawn, a new era of love, peace and joy.

The Angelic Reiki Attunement literally changes our DNA and every cell and molecule in our body; in our consciousness; in our awareness; offering us a connection to the perfection of the Divine. Never before in the history of humanity has it been as possible as it is now to access the higher vibrational worlds, to connect with Celestial beings of Light, the Angelic Kingdom, in order to bring healing to our planet.

By being the channel of Angelic Energy, you are allowing your consciousness to merge with the Divine, helping to bring Divine Mind to earth. By being in the vibration of the Angelic Kingdom of Light, you will experience joy in your life beyond what you have ever experienced before, and beyond what you ever before thought possible.

Through Kevin Core, Archangel Metatron has explained that Angelic Reiki is *"The Healing for our Time"*, simply because, with the recent raising of the earth's vibration, the vibration of the Angelic Kingdom matches this current earth vibration, and therefore resonates strongly with it. Divine Plan always affords us exactly what we need at any given time, and where we are in consciousness is reflected in what is made available to us in the form of Divine assistance.

Angelic Reiki is different from most other forms of healing modalities, in that the practitioner does not have to "do" anything. The whole healing process is given over entirely to the appropriate Angels; the practitioner simply merges the energies and aura of the client with those of the practitioner and of the Angels and holds the sacred space for the Angels to enter and administer the healing. The session ends when the practitioner feels the Angelic energies begin to withdraw.

As in all forms of Reiki, the symbols with which you will be attuned are doorways to higher consciousness and stretch way beyond space and time. The healing arts of ancient times are being re-ignited in these present times through sacred Attunements, bringing in healing and Divine Light to our earth vibration. How beautiful, wonderful and amazing it is that we can assist in the process of Ascension of mankind by these symbols being transmitted through us to enable us to assist all those who wish for help and healing; to enable us to give a helping hand to all as we progress along our own Spiritual path back to Divine Source!

CHAPTER 10

UNICORN REIKI

UNICORN REIKI was one of the first non-traditional Reiki healing energies to be channelled with the special evolution of the earth in 2012. Unicorn Reiki is unique, coming as it does from the mystical, high vibrational, pure Light energies of the Unicorns, who share the same domain as the Angelic Realms. And like Angelic energy, Unicorn energy is filled with pure white Light and unconditional Love. That is all they know.

When you are introduced to the Unicorn energy, you will feel uplifted and remarkable healing will take place. Unicorns will reunite you with your true self and buried life experiences within Atlantis and your past. They will purify and cleanse your thoughts, so you no longer hold onto harmful negative emotions.

The word 'Unicorn' comes from the Latin 'Uni', meaning one, and 'Cornu,' meaning horn. People have believed in Unicorns for centuries. Aristotle, Genghis Khan, Saint Thomas and Saint Gregory believed Unicorns existed. They are featured in the folklore of many cultures and have been known to western cultures for thousands of years. They are mentioned in the Bible many times and there are several references to them in the Old Testament. The Palm Sunday tract in the Roman Catholic missal reads: *"Deliver me from the lion's mouth, and my lowliness from the horns of Unicorns"*.

The Unicorn has always been seen as a symbol of purity, hope, love and majesty. Down through the centuries, belief in these mystical creatures has diminished due to lack of scientific evidence and with people becoming more logical. They have lain dormant and remote for centuries due to mankind not, until now, being ready for Enlightenment. Like the Dragons, Unicorns too are now returning to earth's dimension to help with the raising of the Spiritual consciousness of humanity. Unicorns work with Saint Germain and the Violet Flame, because they resonate with that energy, as both energies originate from Atlantis. Unicorns were in abundance at the time of Atlantis and many times they used the Violet Flame power to heal and rejuvenate.

In heraldry, a Unicorn is depicted as a horse with a goat's cloven hooves and beard, a lion's tail, and a slender, spiral horn on its forehead. Because of its association with Christ, the Unicorn was seemingly too sacred to be widely used in early heraldry, but became popular from the fifteenth century. Two Unicorns support the Scottish Coat of Arms, and a lion and a Unicorn support the English Coat of Arms.

The Unicorn represents purity and a Christ-like connection to God and the Divine. It symbolises your desire and intention to help our planet, its creatures and mankind to achieve purity, by removing negative energy. Generally, Unicorns help people who are more spiritually aware, as these people have their aura and energy on a higher frequency, and so it is easier for the unicorn to reach. The same applies to the healer. Unicorns need the healer to be on the same frequency as they are to channel Unicorn energy directly via the healer's body. This higher frequency is achieved after the Unicorn Reiki Attunement.

Unicorn energy is of a higher vibration than traditional Usui Reiki, and is similar to Angelic healing. Unicorns have the ability to remove negative energy quickly by their strong, swirling energy flow. The healing is usually done by working in the auric field with the practitioner's hands hovering and not touching the client. Unicorn energy works by removing negative energy and opening blockages by using vortex pulse waves, whereas traditional Reiki is a consistent pushing energy, where the healer has to move their hands. Unicorn energy is channelled in a spiral movement, so the practitioner's hands need to remain still. Unicorn energy feels like soft balls of cotton wool, and is often felt moving up the client's arms or down their legs. You may even feel as if you are floating, or that the energy is going into you in circular movements. Everyone is different, so each one feels a unique experience when having Unicorn healing.

The Unicorn Attunement increases the vibrational level of both your Spiritual and physical bodies. It is of a high frequency and is definitely a different energy to traditional Usui Reiki, so you can expect to feel different sensations. The symbols are placed in your auric field so that it is easier for your Unicorn guide to channel energy via your crown chakra and your third eye chakra. The Attunement will increase your energy throughout your body, which has already been activated by your traditional Reiki attunements. The Unicorn healing technique is less complicated than most other healing modalities, as there are less hand positions, and so the healer is able to relax more and go deeper into the healing experience.

The Unicorn healing symbols need to be drawn three times each and pushed into the person's energy field. There are three symbols given to the new practitioner.

First, the '*Karma Symbol*', which removes karma in this or other lives.

Secondly, the '*Guilt Symbol*', which removes guilt, and is used on people who feel lacking in confidence or worry about what other people might think of them.

Finally, the '*Forgiveness Symbol*', which enables people to let go of hurt and move on. It is used for those stuck in a rut and are stubborn or proud, and perhaps holding emotions very deeply, not showing them.

Unicorn healing energy can also be used for distant healing, using the appropriate distant healing symbol.

Unicorns are highly evolved animals. They symbolise a rise in Spiritual consciousness, an increase in Spiritual awareness. The Black Unicorn, however, further symbolises that this increase in Spiritual consciousnes has not yet been understood by the person involved. All Unicorns are highly intelligent and work alongside Lightworkers in clearing negative energy and rescuing human and animal souls.

Unicorn healing is a truly beautiful energy with which to work. Unicorns are not like us. They do not think like us and are not analytical like us. So go with your instinct, not your logic. Trust what you sense and feel. Look out for large white feathers,- a sign from your Unicorn. Small white feathers are a sign from the Angels. Know that your Unicorns are with you for life once you have been attuned to their energy, and enjoy the wonderful Spiritual experiences they will bring to you!

As Lewis Carroll wrote: *"Well, now that we have seen each other"*, said the *Unicorn, "if you'll believe in me, I'll believe in you. Is that a bargain?"*

CHAPTER 11

PEGASUS REIKI

PEGASUS REIKI energy, like all Unicorn energy, comes from the same vibration as the Archangels, and so is very powerful, with only Master healers able to channel it. It is a recently evolved energy, with the healer rarely touching the client because the Reiki energy is channelled into the auric field.

With the galactic re-alignment in 2012, there has been a raising of the vibrations of the planets in our solar system, enabling Spiritual beings such as Ascended Masters, Archangels and Pegasus to work closer to the physical earth plane and help Lightworkers.

Pegasus Master Reiki Attunement joins you with a unicorn herd. Welcome them into your life for positivity, love and abundance. Pegasus Reiki will bring you inner peace, wisdom, and closer to the Angelic and Unicorn Kingdoms.

The name "Pegasus" in Greek translates as 'Fountain Horse'. Pegasus is a white, winged, Spiritual horse who is the leader of the mystical Unicorns and the animal kingdom. Very old and very wise, Pegasus is often sought out for advice by Unicorns, Archangels, Ascended Masters and the Lords of Karma. His energy is so pure, coming directly from Source, making him unique. He projects his thoughts intuitively to the Unicorns on the earth plane and co-ordinates their work in clearing the planet of negative energy. Pegasus also communicates telepathically with humans.

His Spiritual realm is in the outer layer of the earth, in the cosmos, where, until now, he has been unable to remain for periods of time due to the heavy, etheric, earth layer. This was because his vibrational energy is so high that he found it difficult to lower his vibration to descend down to the denser, physical, earth realm. 2012 started a healing shift for our earth and so Pegasus has had to wait for the healing to lift negative energy to the surface. In 2013, Lemurian crystals buried within the earth centuries ago began to be re-activated, and this too also helped clear deep rooted, negative earth energy. The earth is now settling, with only pockets of negativity, and this has enabled Pegasus to venture into these new less dense etheric layers surrounding the earth. This means that Pegasus is now able to descend down to our physical earth realm and to channel his energy directly through Lightworkers and Unicorns.

Up until 2012, Pegasus was the only winged horse, all other Unicorns being wingless. Now newly evolved Unicorns, complete with wings, their energy channelled directly from Pegasus, have emerged to assist Pegasus with healing the earth and helping animals to evolve. Their presence is so powerful, a mass of pure Divine Light, that all lower energies are defenceless against them. You might feel their energy as a very cold draught coming in around your feet and ankles.

Pegasus works with Divine Light which is so powerful that it defuses any negative particles and transmutes them into light. Every being, good and not-so-good, started from the Light Source and as such, their original form was of the Light. Pegasus Reiki transforms and dissolves negativity, so releasing blockages. Even self-sabotage feelings of guilt are released and transformed into positive thinking of love and self-worth. Pegasus Reiki resolves issues of self-destruct where people have addictive problems or abuse themselves or others. Pegasus energy helps the inner child, the original soul energy, to feel loved so they feel supported and not alone. Most addictions or cases of abuse are a cry for help from the soul feeling lost and depressed.

Pegasus Reiki, like all Unicorn Reiki, is different from other forms of Reiki in that it is mainly done at the client's head, with the practitioner working within the auric field. The healing clears a passage through the aura, using the directional flow of the crown chakra. Healing the auric field clears blockages in the chakras of the physical body and the emotional, mental and Ascension, etheric layers. The physical body is receiving healing when the etheric auric bodies are cleared. The healing radiates outwards into the auric field with the healer building up strong energy within the first three auric layers. The healer works on the first auric layer, the etheric body, starting at the head, until this layer is strong; then moves to the next layer, the emotional body; then working through the mental body and finally the Ascension body, until all the four auric layers have been repaired and replenished.

The etheric body is the first auric layer surrounding the physical body. Healing of the physical body is related to the base chakra. It is the lowest vibrational level which connects the physical body to the higher bodies. Healing this auric field realigns chakras by cleansing and removing physical blockages.

The emotional body is the second auric layer surrounding the physical body, next to the etheric body. This emotional body is associated with our feelings about ourselves. Healing on this level is usually pink to generate unconditional love. This auric layer is connected to the sacral chakra and is associated with the heart chakra. Healing this auric field creates loving energy to deflect negativity; increase self-worth and brings inner peace and an acceptance of one's self.

The mental body is the third auric layer. This is associated with the vibrational level of thoughts and logic. It is connected to the solar plexus chakra, where buried thought forms are stored. Healing this auric layer removes negative karmic patterns to allow positive thoughts to surface. It helps people to accept that life's decisions have been made for a reason.

Finally, the Ascensional body is the fourth auric layer surrounding the physical body. This is the Ascension soul or higher self, where the soul is connected to Ascended Masters, the White Brotherhood, and Lords of Karma. The White Brotherhood are a group of highly evolved beings, dedicated to bringing Divine Light to earth. Healing this auric layer empowers Spiritual people to use their gifts; awaken their intuitive message system, and let go of logic to allow Spiritual guidance to be received.

Pegasus Master healers will often feel freezing forearms, wrists and hands. The energy of Pegasus is so strong that it is channelled into the healer's auric field as well as via the chakras, out through their palm chakras. The healer invariably will feel as if they are in a column of energy, so will feel their auric field tingle with cold waves and pulses. Pegasus Reiki heals both the client and the healer at the same time; the more often the healer practises Pegasus Reiki, the healthier they will become emotionally, mentally, physically, and of course spiritually.

A healer who has been attuned to the Pegasus Reiki has a permanent connection to Pegasus through an etheric cord. The Attunement makes the bonding extra special as Pegasus is now permanently joined with you mentally and spiritually. This etheric cord is attached next to and alongside the crown chakra; this is how Pegasus channels his power to you.

Pegasus Master Reiki has five symbols, to be used when the healer intuitively feels the need for them.

First, the *'Pegasus Master Symbol'*, which is a very powerful but effective cleanser of negativity. It increases the energy of Pegasus Reiki, used in healing, for protection and for opening communication portals.

Secondly, the '*Severance Symbol*', which dissolves, splits or severs negative, etheric cords.

Thirdly, the '*Rectification Symbol*', which is placed within the auric field to shield against psychic attack or self-harm. It is like a good bacteria which travels around eating all the bad bacteria.

Fourthly, the '*Ascension Symbol*', which lifts the soul by increasing vibrational energy, and is also very effective in helping to deal with stress related issues.

Finally, the '*Containment Symbol*', which affords Spiritual help and support to Lightworkers. This symbol extracts light energy from the earth which connects to the soul, so they feel safe, secure and belonging here on the earth plane.

Pegasus Reiki works in cold pulses and waves, coming out of the hands of the healer in soft spiral movements, feeling a bit like soft cotton wool, and systematically using the flow of the auric field to travel to the higher self. It can be use for self-healing and distance healing as well as presence healing on other people and animals.

After your Attunement to Pegasus Reiki, your Unicorns will take you on life journeys where you meet others whom either you yourself need, or who may need you. Pegasus will ensure you always have what you need, surrounding you in gentle loving wings, and bringing you love, happiness and abundance.

CHAPTER 12

DOLPHIN REIKI

DOLPHIN REIKI is a powerful energy which is very different from traditional Reiki. This is because traditional Reiki is a static, constant movement, whereas Dolphin Reiki moves in pulse waves. It is important for the practitioner to maintain steady hands when giving Dolphin healing, as the Dolphin energy is using the practitioner's stationary palm chakra to pulsate energy, and any movement of the hands would interrupt that flow of energy.

Everything in creation is held together through the most elaborate, the most intricate, the most exquisite system of geometrical and mathematical equations and sound vibrations. The specific sounds that both whales and dolphins create and the specific sound vibrations they emit, play a major part in holding our planet together. They have a very special place on our planet, as they have the ability to communicate on a higher, Spiritual level. Their psychic ability is very intense; they are of the highest intelligence; are able to communicate and interact with people and can learn to perform the most difficult of tasks. They can help children with special needs and have often been known to rescue those in difficulty at sea. They have a universal appeal, symbolising joy, freedom, grace and serenity. But, like humans, they can also have mood swings!

We all have different physical shapes. Dolphins are another version of humans, existing in many dimensions at the same time. Their playful, joyous nature is sourced in a very highly evolved consciousness that knows it is eternal; knows it will never be destroyed or ended; and it has a deep bonding with us, its human counterpart,- we who have forgotten that we are eternal and infinite

Spiritual beings. They have a great love of people, and because of this, they want to help us on our path to Enlightenment. On a higher level, they have agreed to teach mankind the importance of love and forgiveness. Their souls have been assigned to bring healing and psychic power to people who interact with them. Their healing role is similar to that of the Angelic realms and Unicorns, and like the Angelic and Unicorn energies, the Dolphin's healing energy can transcend time, space and different Spiritual dimensions to go wherever it is required.

Dolphins are descendants of ancient beings from various stars and galaxies, such as Sirius and the Pleiades, and they are here to transfer to us the ancient truths and wisdom for preserving and loving our planet earth. Dolphins live in a connected consciousness, which extends beyond themselves to each other and beyond planet earth to their home planet, Sirius, the planet of their origin. Their aura exudes an energy that can heal, as well as accept, process and pass on information. For aeons of time, they have carried frequencies from many of our ancient civilizations. The Dolphins that existed during the Age of Atlantis were coded and programmed to pass on, genetically and telepathically, information to the human species. Their message is clear. They are currently leaving our planet in great numbers. And why? Simply because their quality of life is rapidly deteriorating here. And what is their message through all of this? Their message to us is that if their quality of life is in jeopardy, then so too is ours! They are a mirror image of ourselves. They are leaving, with the message to us that it is now time for us to take stewardship of our own planet! To take responsibility for our own actions!

Animals are not stupid. Far from it! They know they never cease to exist. They know they only change form when they pass over. And they know there is a new world in the process of forming. Many species are becoming extinct, not just because they have become victims of man's greed and lust for power over them, but because they are actually in the process of moving into the 'Vibrational Corridor' to advance into a higher vibrational frequency, the higher vibrational frequency of the New Earth that is emerging as the old earth expires.

Spiritual Atlantis Dolphins work on healing and repairing the body's spiritual, mental and soul energy, using sonar energy waves which resonate with sound. Their healing is unique in that they work within the cosmic energy field of the planet, using this cosmic energy to heal karma and emotional damage so the Soul can evolve. You will most probably feel a sense of dizziness or movement as if on water when working with Dolphin energy, due to them circling and 'swimming' around you. Their energy comes in waves and is felt as a mixture of tingles, hot and cold pulses, which is very different to other healing Reiki types.

 An increase in your soul vibrational level will have already been activated by your traditional Reiki attunements. This Dolphin Attunement will now further increase that vibrational level throughout your body, and you will need to ground yourself more. You may find that your head, crown, forehead and scalp are more sensitive. You may also feel your Dolphin healing pod around you at night time or when you are resting. This is so they can get used to your earth body and your soul. You may even feel a little floaty, as if you are on water.

You will most definitely feel more compassionate and loving; you will go with the flow more and you will have an increased sense of fun and enjoyment in life.

There are three symbols given to the new practioner at the Attunement process. These symbols are very intense and strong, and need only be drawn once. They should not be used on Spiritually closed people.

The first symbol, the '*Wholeness Symbol*', brings the person's soul, higher self, mental and physical body into alignment, bringing harmony, peace and life fulfilment.

The second symbol, the '*Cosmos Symbol*', represents universe energy above and solid energy below. It draws in the energy of the higher realms, your guides, Angels, universe and cosmos, heightening your psychic ability. It has the same frequency as the traditional Reiki Power Symbol or pure Love Symbol. It can be used to heal the ocean, moon, or even the sun, as well as people, places and animals. This symbol resonates with Archangels Metatron and Sandalphon: call on Metatron for personal everyday problems and Sandalphon for larger scale problems which involve a group of people or organisation.

The third symbol is the '*Source Symbol*', and is used when going through an emotional transitional period, such as redundancy, divorce, moving house etc. It can also be used to help the planet, universe and higher realms in their evolution to reach Ascension.

As each individual gains Enlightenment and makes the shift into a more connected and expansive awareness, a more connected and expansive consciousness, human-kind will experience a greater understanding, a greater Oneness, a greater connectedness with the dolphins. They were developed by intelligent beings with a different kind of consciousness from that of humans, to survive and thrive on planet earth in the oceans instead of on land. Their technology is a mental technology, unlike the physical technology developed by humans.

The gift of Atlantean Healing Dolphin energy will transform your life in many ways. You will certainly feel more drawn to Nature and to water. Your Dolphins will surround you with their love and understanding, as the universe watches over you, bringing you inner peace and beautiful new, Spiritual experiences.

CHAPTER 13

ELEMENTAL REIKI

ELEMENTAL Reiki is a unique healing modality that beautifully combines the healing energy of the fairies and other elemental beings. This course will open your energy to the frequency of the elemental kingdom so you will become as one of them. Healing with the elementals is special because you will be helping the environment as well as animals and people.

The elemental kingdom is comprised of many types of fairies, gnomes, pixies and others but they fall into four main groups. The group they are in will depend on what material and element they resonate with. The elemental group works and heals using the energy of water, fire, soil or air, and has an influence on everything we walk on and the air we breathe.

Earth and air elementals work together when healing, as their combined frequencies are able to penetrate deeper when healing a person or animal. The earth elemental frequency resonates with crystals, soil, sand, gemstones, rocks, stones and the earth, whereas the air elementals are natural healers, helping animals and plants.

The earth and air elementals are cheeky, curious, eager to learn and playful. They look like Tinkerbell, and tend to play around a healer's head, making their nose itch with their wings gently touching the face. They have transparent wings and bodies which change colour depending on where they are and what they are doing. Healing with the earth and air elementals changes, depending on whether the need is for heavier energy to be removed, or lighter energy to raise frequency. These combined groups work usually on chakras, the auric field and emotions. At the start of a healing session clients may feel like they want to sneeze or that they have bubbles up their nose, like when having a glass of champagne. This is the earth and air fairies working on the crown chakra and then the third eye. When the healing travels down to the throat chakra, the person may feel like coughing as the fairies work to release any emotional and physical blockages. These sensations usually don't last long once the fairies have managed to create a healing channel so their healing can surge down to the feet.

Undines, water sprites and sylphs are the elemental fairies that work and heal using the power of water. Water elementals heal the soul and higher self.

Salamanders are the elementals who work using the power of fire, moving within the fire energy. They are the most unpredictable and temperamental healers, but their energy is immensely powerful. The fire Elementals heal the physical body and bring protection.

Elemental Reiki uses eight symbols derived from Goddess, Elemental and Pagan energy. All Reiki symbols are able to be signed with others from different Reiki types, for example, Angel, Dragon, Unicorn, Dolphin, Golden Eagle etc. Many of the Elemental Symbols do not have a correct way of signing them except with bringing the energy from above and down towards earth. Each symbol needs to be signed only once.

The '*Spirit Symbol*' represents the Oneness of the universe with man. It is all that we are, were, and ever could be. It is the never-ending cycle of death and rebirth. This symbol is for healing any and all afflictions to do with a Spiritual nature. It brings people back to the here and now, to face their problems, and gives them direction in what they need to do. The energy of the Spirit symbol awakens the soul to help the physical mind and body cope with life's issues.

The '*Water Symbol*' represents love, emotions, feelings, nurturing and balance in times of change. This symbol helps with healing involving an emotional nature, or balancing stress or anxiety problems.

The '*Fire Symbol*' grounds and seals the newly awakened Reiki energies, and so is drawn downwards from the heavens to the earth. It brings in inner and physical strength to increase confidence and self-worth, so the person is no longer a victim, and helps people who have addictions to go to the core of the problem.

The '*Air Symbol*' represents the 'breath of life' using the elemental power of movement in the air. It is for use on people who are not being honest or truthful to themselves, those with a blocked throat chakra, as they are unable to express themselves. This symbol awakens ideas by giving clarity of thought and honesty, so people see the clearer picture. It is also good to use on soft tissue injuries, and especially clients with asthma or those recovering from a chest infection.

The '*Earth Symbol*' represents Mother Goddess energy. The energy of this symbol connects us to Nature by grounding us and helping us feel supported and soothed. It is for use in slowing down chakras that are spinning too fast or are too open. It is signed into the crown chakra or third eye to help an anxious person or a child with ADHD to become calm.

The 'Comfort Symbol', a gentle and compassionate energy, is for emotional problems and so is only to be used on the throat and heart chakras. If used by mistake on the solar plexus, it may make the client angry with the symbol bringing up buried anger caused by emotional hurt. It cannot, of course, be signed incorrectly, as your guides are always in control. It brings comfort to those dealing with dramatic life changes, for example bereavement, separation, redundancy, retirement, financial debt, crime or betrayal.

The '*Growth Symbol* 'is only to be used on the lower three chakras,- the solar plexus, sacral and base. This symbol converts negative particles into light, and so eats away at negativity. It is for use on those with bad backs, hip, knee or ankle problems.

The '*Eternal Love Symbol*' brings in Divine Love of the elementals, Angels and Unicorns. It increases protection with its gold energy, as all lower energies are repelled by love. This beautiful symbol brings in love to everyone.

Finally, the '*Elemental Master Symbol*' is for practitioners' use only, for those attuned to Elemental Reiki. Its purpose is to increase your elemental Reiki power for all elemental disciplines of healing. It can be signed on your pillow before you go to sleep or on the back of the chair before you begin your meditation.

Once you have been attuned, the Elemental Reiki will be with you always, so your Guides will help you see the Light in any negative situations. People will be drawn to your fairy energy, especially children and animals. Your home will be filled with fun and love from the elemental kingdom. The child in you will be brought out, opening your heart to joy and happiness.

CHAPTER 14

DRAGON CRYSTAL REIKI

DRAGON CRYSTAL REIKI is a strong healing energy, one of the most recent modalities to be introduced to us here on planet earth.

Dragons have been around the earth plane for many thousands of years, but it is only now that we are starting to feel them, however, due to the raising of the vibration of our planet. They have always lived amongst us, on a higher vibrational level, hence we have not realised their presence. They come from Spirit and have never existed in the physical realms, only in the Spiritual realms of the other worlds.

Science has taught us that we need to see or hear before we can accept something as real. However, increasing numbers of people have no difficulty in believing in Angels or even Unicorns, despite the fact that they do not see them, but when it comes to believing in Dragons, there is still a great hesitation, a great doubting, a great apprehension.

Where do Dragons come from?

The cradle of civilization is now considered by most experts to be that of the ancient Sumerians. The Sumerians flourished about six thousand years ago in Mesopotamia, an area located between the Tigris and Euphrates rivers, now known as Iraq and Kuwait. The Sumerian culture was seeded by beings from star galaxies, the stellar reptilian ancestors. They were experimenting, like many other groups of beings from different vibrational energy levels, and investigating if life could be lived on planet earth.

Dragons, serpents and reptilian visitors to earth have featured in ancient myths and legends for hundreds of thousands of years, these stories conveyed orally down through succeeding generations. Much later, these were captured by the Sumerians on their cylinder seals, devices that recorded selected information in pictorial form.

Diverse cultures right across the globe embrace the idea of dragons or serpents as the creators of life. The Aborigines, the Mayans, the Native peoples of North and South America, cultures throughout Africa and Asia,- all acknowledge the existence of reptilian life as being fundamental and basic in our story of human development and evolution. Serpents, dragons and reptiles underpin the principal teachings and beliefs of almost every indigenous culture. They are used as ritual symbols, and as an acknowledgement of where people have come from. Even Saint Patrick, when he came to Ireland, is reported to have banished the snakes from this country!

Dragons were feared by many because they could breathe fire but they were mostly credited with bringing power, life and prosperity.

The reptilian energies are an ancient life-form and were some of the prime instigators in creating the human species on planet earth. They were brilliant at genetic manipulation and organisation, and with their great ability to genetically adjust life, they were able to not only survive, but to thrive on planet earth, within the unique biological forces that earth presented.

As the peoples on earth lost their connection to Divine Source, and fell further and further into individualism and separation from each other in order to gain power, egotistical materialism and depravity took over. As a consequence, species of animal life exited this vibrational level, no longer able to live alongside lower and more dense forms of energy. Unicorns and Dragons all left the consciousness awareness of humanity.

Today, however, with the raising of the earth's vibration and the thinning of the veils between worlds, we are being forced to acknowledge the vast uniqueness of Divine intelligence, as different forms of life energy reveal themselves to us, clearing away the barriers to inner truths.

Dragons are returning once again, like other forms of life energy, to our human consciousness awareness. They are making their presence known in movies, television, books, advertisements. They are depicted as kind, helpful, wise and benevolent, as well as knowledgeable and wise, and are currently enjoying a new-found surge of popularity with younger people.

The ancient reptiles that we call dragons sometimes hoarded crystals. Crystals, for earlier civilizations, were receivers and senders of messages and a source of power. Within these crystals were stored all sorts of inner information and blue-prints. Many of the highest civilizations were anchored by reptilian energies, who brought a great amount of crystal energy, transferring information from one system to another. They then sent versions of themselves as snakes, into the outside world, carrying this coded information. Had they appeared as dragons, human consciousness at that time would not have been able to withstand the encounter.

In China, today, as for many centuries, dragons are a good fortune symbol. The symbol of the dragon is said to generate cosmic Chi that brings wealth, luck and good fortune, as well as offering protection against illness, accidents and lower energies.

The legend of the dragon symbol in Wales has been well documented. Ancient Welsh scholars used the dragon to symbolise famous leaders or formidable warriors. The title 'Pendragon', meaning 'Head Dragon', was given to ancient, great kings and leaders. King Arthur's father was known as Uther Pendragon. It was believed that having the title of the dragon gave them power to defeat their enemies.

The legend of the White and Red Dragons came to symbolise the struggle between the Welsh and the English. Eventually the Welsh Red Dragon triumphed over the English White Dragon, and after the Battle of Bosworth in 1485, the Red Dragon became established as the symbol of the Welsh people by Henry Tudor. He used the Red Dragon on a green and white background to represent his claim to be one of the ancient Kings of Britain and as an acknowledgement to the Welsh who had made the victory over Richard The Third possible.

In 1501, the Red Dragon officially became recognised as the symbol of Wales. The design for the Welsh flag was accepted in 1953 and received the Royal Assent from Queen Elizabeth The Second in 1959.

Dragon Reiki is becoming popular due to off-planet, higher vibrational energies, raising the vibration of the earth, and is here to help with the earth's Spiritual evolutionary process. While the traditional Usui Reiki was initiated in Japan in the 1800s where the ancient healing technique of Jesus was rediscovered, in China, Dragon Reiki was developed by practitioners of Japanese-based Reiki who combined the energy of the dragon with the deep healing of Nature.

Dragon Reiki teaches that healing begins within the individual, on a spiritual level, before healing the physical; the mental and spiritual well-being of a person dictates the physical condition. Dragon energy also acts as a protector and source of strength. Dragons clear negative energies and bring powerful Spiritual healing.

Spiritual Dragons live peacefully on our earth dimension, within the middle etheric layer, though on a different vibrational level from us. They are not timid or shy, but are very wary of humans, due to the fact that we store so much negative energy. Like Unicorns, dragons are pure Light energy, and they are involved mainly in assisting Unicorns and the Angelic and elemental kingdoms in cleansing our environment of lower, negative energy forces. Their white fire breath is used to cleanse a room or building or to cleanse the aura of the person with whom it works, so that person's energy is maintained at a high intensity.

Dragons are strong, helpful, intelligent and wise. They are the most courageous and the bravest forces of the ethereal realms in the fight against lower forces. They are the guardians of sacred knowledge and symbols.

When working with your dragon energy, you will possibly feel cold above your head and waves of warm and cold through your body and hand chakras. Your dragon's white breath will cleanse the aura of your client, in preparation for the healing. Dragon energy is usually felt in pulses, and, in your hands can feel like sand or a gritty sensation, as if you are rubbing your hands against bubble-wrap.

Dragon symbols only require to be drawn once. The new practitioner is given four symbols.

First, the 'Dragon's Heart Key', which brings harmony and balance. It can be used to clear and transform negative energy into white Light, and also for protection.

Secondly, the 'Transformation Symbol', which is used to bring about change or clearance of a problem or situation. It helps people who are stressed to make positive changes in their life. This symbol is similar to the Reiki Power Symbol, so is very strong.

Thirdly, the '*Balance Symbol*', which is useful for realigning your chakras, especially your third eye and throat chakra. This symbol helps people to open up and be more honest and truthful.

Fourthly, the '*Unity Symbol*', which is used in deep meditation to connect with your higher self, and to connect your guides and Spiritual helpers with your physical body, mind and soul. This symbol reinforces your life's purpose and helps you to remain on the right path and not be persuaded by outsiders to change your direction. It also helps you to accept who you are, and to be proud of who you are. In addition to these four symbols, the new practitioner is given the' *Unification Symbol*', for personal use. This symbol represents the joining of two different powers, human and Dragon, to be united, making a stronger connection between you and your Dragon.

With your Dragon's help, you will be able to clear the earth, your friends, family, and of course, yourself of any negative energy. Life will certainly be more exciting with your dragon beside you. There will, of course, be obstacles to face, that is the nature of life, but you will have the reassurance that your loyal Dragon will be protecting you. Life is very precious, and is what we each make of it for ourselves. All things happen for a reason, and all bad happenings have a happy outcome. Try and let go of logic and reasoning, so your guides and especially your Dragon, can give you guidance and support.

CHAPTER 15

GOLDEN EAGLE REIKI

GOLDEN EAGLE REIKI is a healing modality from the Native American tradition, channelled directly from Great White Spirit, through Ascended Master, Lord Melchizedek, down to the Stone Lodge Elders of the Native Americans.

All of the numerous tribes,- Cherokee, Blackfoot, Cheyenne, Sioux, Apache, to name but a few, had similar beliefs, in that they believed in The Great White Spirit (God/Source); Mother Earth, the giver of life; connection with all forms of life, animal, mineral, plant and the healing properties of the natural plants and foliage around them. Their respect for Mother Earth, all in her and on her was total and absolute. The buffalo was killed only when required, and no part of it was wasted. Everything they needed was got from the buffalo and the natural vegetation around them.

Native Americans were in constant communication with the animal and bird kingdoms; the four-legged and the winged ones. As Chief Dan George taught: "*If you talk to the animals / they will talk to you / and you will know each other. / If you do not talk to them / you will not know them / and what you do not know / you will fear. / What one fears, one destroys.*"

The Golden Eagle was believed by the Native Americans to have spiritual powers. A huge bird, awesome in its presence, the eagle flies high above the earth, seeing the complete landscape. It has no concept of fear, as other animals, even the birds, are its prey. Eagles are a preserved species in North America, and even an eagle's feather is sacred to the Native Americans; it cannot be taken or owned by anyone outside of the Native American tradition.

During the Golden Eagle Reiki practitioner course, you will be introduced to the Native American way of life, their customs and traditions. The importance to them of the earth, the four winds, the sun, sunrise, sunset, the moon, the stars, the sweat lodge, feather healing, animal spirit guides, the winged ones, peace pipe, totem pole, pow-wow, medicine wheel, meditation, quieting the mind in order to allow healing, will all be explained. As will the Native American Ten Commandments:

- The Earth is our Mother; care for her.

- Honour all your relations.

- Open your heart and soul to the Great Spirit.

- All life is sacred, treat all beings with respect.

- Take from the earth what is needed and nothing more.

- Do what needs to be done for the good of all.

- Give constant thanks to the Great Spirit for every day.

- Speak the truth but only of the good of others.

- Follow the rhythms of nature: rise and retire with the sun.

- Enjoy life's journey, but leave no tracks.

Your Native American guides will join you several days prior to your Attunement. Our Native Indian guides are very much like what they were when they lived on this earth plane. They are proud, respectful and stand no nonsense. They understand that healing is not just about repairing, cleansing and realigning our physical body, but also healing the mind and especially the soul. They see energy within every living thing, and all living things are as One in Great White Spirit. Everything needs to be balanced, including our way of life, our education, our family and our enjoyment. If we can achieve balance, we can become One with Source.

Native Indian Guides are very proud and traditional. They are not interested in politics of any kind, political, family or work. They see all mankind as part of the bigger picture and not with mundane, earthly worries. They have a calming presence and help healers to remain unfazed by life's hurdles. They prevent negative thoughts or actions from taking hold within the healer. They have amazing patience and grace and their way of showing displeasure is to disappear from the scene of an argument, returning when the situation has calmed.

The Golden Eagle Reiki Attunement opens your base and root chakras to connect you to Lady Gaia (Mother Earth), the earth's golden ray energy within the earth's center. The earth has increased her vibration with the connection with the other planets in our solar system in 2012, an energy that occurs only every few thousand years. This increased vibration is releasing a new energy of the Golden Ray, a Spiritual power of which the Mayans, Aztecs and Egyptians were very aware, possibly due to the influence of the teachings of the Pleiadians. The Golden Eagle Reiki Attunement is the golden energy of the earth which has been released to help our planet reach Enlightenment.

There are four symbols attached to this Attunement. Each symbol needs to be drawn three times as they all invoke energy of Mother Earth, Golden Ray vibration. They can be signed over any of the chakras and used on their own or with other Reiki symbols. These symbols resonate and work well with children, animals and Mother

Nature. They are powerful and uncomplicated and do not need to be drawn in any particular way or placed in any particular direction. Each has its own unique energy and the vibration may change, depending on whether you are working with your Native Indian guide or your power guide.

The first symbol, the '*Messenger Symbol*', is used when help is needed for abundance, guidance, and for calling in answers. The answer will come through what you see, hear or feel, for example through what someone says to you, pictures, music, signs in shop windows, etc. Remember! Nothing ever happens at random! Everything is synchronised! This symbol is good for clients who feel lacking in confidence, or feel they are unworthy to ask for help.

Secondly, the '*Peace Symbol*' ,which brings in earth Golden Ray energy to life and energises physical and Spiritual power. It helps those who are stressed or anxious, or with a troubled mind, and also helps negative people to believe in good things.

The third symbol, the '*Four Winds Symbol*', helps the client to see the picture clearly from all angles, and brings life balance in work and play. It is useful for those who are stubborn, stuck in the past or are unwilling to change. It is also good for those who feel guilty and need to release.

Fourthly, the '*Golden Feather Symbol*', creates protective energy with positive power. It is used to shield yourself, by thought or signing three times. It is good for use on people who enjoy being a victim or have lost faith in themselves.

After your Golden Eagle Reiki Attunement, you will see the world as a place of great joy, finding peace and fulfilment within every tree, plant, animal and person. Be confident and assured that you are helping others to find contentment and happiness within themselves, and that your Native Indian guides are walking alongside you, keeping you strong and on your right path.

And as you journey with them, remember the words of Chief Tecumesh: "*Live your life that the fear of death can never enter your heart. / Trouble no one about his religion. / Respect others in their views and demand that they respect yours. / Love your life, perfect your life, beautify all things in your life. / Seek to make your life long and of service to your people. / Prepare a noble death song for the day when you go over the great divide. / Always give a word or sign of salute when meeting or passing a friend, / or even a stranger, if in a lonely place. / Show respect to all people, but grovel to none. / When you rise in the morning, give thanks for the light, / for your life, for your strength. / Give thanks for your food and for the joy of living. / If you see no reason to give thanks, the fault lies in yourself. / Abuse no one and no thing, for abuse turns the wise ones to fools / and robs the spirit of its vision.*"

And if only we could all apply the following prayer of the Americal Indians, what a peaceful, joyful world this would be: "*O Great Spirit / Let your voice whisper righteousness in our ears through the west wind in the late of the day. / Let us be comforted with love for our brothers and sisters with no war. / Let us hold good health mentally and physically, to solve our problems / and accomplish something for future generations of life. / Let us be sincere to ourselves and our youth and make the world a better place to live.*"

CHAPTER 16

GODDESS OF LIGHT REIKI

GODDESS OF LIGHT REIKI is another unique energy that has awakened with the onset of the new global energy that was activated in 2012. It is one of the strongest current energies, and it is only now that people are able to channel its purest form to its full potential. Previously, we were limited, not only with our physical bodies, but also with the heaviness of the earth's negative energies, which have been absorbed over many thousands of years. With the recent planetary alignment, earth has been able to dislodge negative energy and cleanse herself. With the earth having a Spiritual cleansing, the White Light is at its strongest on the earth plane, with smaller pockets of negative energy.

Goddess of Light Reiki is special because the Goddess Light beings work with the pure Light energy of the Heavens, and now because of the earth's new, higher Spiritual frequency, the Goddesses have been assigned special tasks in order to assist all on earth to achieve Spiritual Enlightenment.

The Goddesses of Light are highly evolved female Light beings who have not been in a physical form for thousands of years. They are female beings who use their female influence to channel the Spiritual power of the White light. The Goddess of Light Reiki high-frequency energy penetrates deep within the physical body to heal the mind and soul. This powerful Light Ray energy is able to increase vibration to dispel negative thought patterns so the individual increases self confidence, self esteem and well-being. The Goddesses of Light want to help you in all areas of your life, whether relationships, work, or problems with life in general. They have a strong belief that for you to be happy, all things need to be settled. Even the smallest mundane thing can eventually grow and become a massive problem. So they will intervene and influence you on any decisions you need to make.

At present, there are only four Goddesses of Light, but just like the Archangels and the Ascended Masters, many more will be enrolled in the near future, as they too, just like us, progress on their path of Ascension and increased Spiritual consciousness. They are independent Light beings who are directly overseen by Source and Archangel Sandalphon. Archangel Sandalphon and Archangel Metatron are the only two Archangels who were once embodied in a physical body, Sandalphon as the prophet *Elijah* and Metatron as the wise scribe *Enoch*.

The Goddesses have been given Divine permission for the first time ever to intervene and influence any aspect of human life. They have to use their own wisdom and judgement as to how much they interfere. They are independent from the Archangels and Ascended Masters, so this means they are only accountable directly to Source. All other beings including Archangels and Ascended Masters will not interfere unless we ask or are in mortal danger, whereas the Goddesses will step in without our requesting them to do so, but will still at the same time respect our point of view and our free will. Previously all beings were left alone to learn by their mistakes and develop Spiritually without too much intervention from higher sources, but Divine Source now feels humans are ready to have Divine help in all areas without waiting for us to request assistance.

Currently the four Goddesses are *Amerissis, Theia, Athena* and *Artemis*.

Goddess Amerissis was the first to ascend to this status. She has two main roles. First, she is Chohan of the Light Ray of Ascension.

Secondly, she is holder of the Secret Ray of Akash, and as such, she holds etheric keys to the scrolls of lifetime experiences. Amerissis uses her power to heal with the influence of water, using water to cleanse the oceans and the rain to wash away negative energy. She helps people to communicate with their Spirit Guides, and spends time evaluating, assessing and intimating to our guides how they can best help us.

Goddess Theia is the Chohan of the Light Ray of Divine Sight, the Sun and the Earth. Her role is to help us to develop our intuitive thoughts and to awaken our Spiritual senses. Theia works with the energy of the sun during the day and the energy of the moon, early morning or late afternoon, with her energy being more powerful during full moon at night time. Theia communicates with our Guardian Angel about how best to help us. She encourages Lightworkers to use their instinct and inner feelings in all aspects of our spiritual work, and uses her influence to teach us to always follow our first thought and not place logic in the way to cloud our judgment. She ensures our souls are strong and filled with love, so our inner self can support us in times of stress, sadness or loss. She will comfort the soul of a Lightworker just before passing to the next realm and in some cases will accompany them to the Halls of Learning and the Lords of Karma life review. Theia uses the Light Ray to connect with our heart chakra to cleanse and open to the love of the Divine. Love is the strongest and purest energy, against which the lower vibrational energies have no defense.

Goddess Artemis is Chohan of the Light Ray of Protection, protecting both people and animals, and works with Pegasus and the Unicorns as well as the Lightworker's animal power guides. Her auric field is surrounded by animal souls which she is protecting and taking to the Light for safety. Her new role is to use the Light to illuminate the darkness.

Goddess Athena is the Chohan of the Light Ray of Philosophy and Wisdom. Her name means 'wise'. She is a Goddess of war strategy, influencing us to use other means than war to settle arguments. When there is a clash of light and dark energies, Athena is there to keep the peace so that resolutions can be worked out in a passive way. She is usually accompanied by an owl, who helps her to search in the darkness and watch over people and animals while they sleep. She guards the 'empty' body while the soul is astra travelling or on dream journeys. She will teach us logic in our dreams and how to control our thoughts and actions while we dream.

There are six symbols included in this modality. With the Goddess of Light Reiki frequency being a recent vibrational power, the symbols contain a higher frequency and so need to be signed only once. Also with the Goddess Reiki working on the client's heart, mind and higher self, the symbols are signed above the head where the soul star chakra is located.

The first symbol, the *Foresight Symbol'*, is very powerful so can only be used on Master clients. This symbol opens up the soul star chakra to allow connection with your higher self, and increases inner Goddess power to overcome problems such as stress, ill health and bereavement. It works on all levels, mentally, physically, spiritually and the higher self.

The second symbol, the *Inner Sanctum'*, helps with clients who are depressed or who have self-destruct tendencies. It gives support to the Higher Self so Higher Self does not weaken with the negative energy the person is producing.

The third symbol, the *Falsehood Symbol'*, is very effective at getting the client to be honest and seek what they truly need. It helps the person to love themselves so that they know they deserve only the best, and therefore desire only the best for themselves.

The fourth symbol, the '*Manifestation Symbol*', is useful when someone is under psychic attack from a jealous or envious person. The jealous person will then be sent a positive energy as a blessing so they no longer feel envious or threatened. This symbol increases confidence, self-worth, a sense of humour and fun. It also helps those who are too serious or work too hard, no longer enjoying life as they should. A good symbol to place on business cards, greeting cards or photographs, as it makes people feel happy.

The fifth symbol, the '*Deity Symbol*', is for the practitioner's use only, and not for the client, as it intensifies the Goddess of Light energy for personal healing and meditation. It awakens the Goddess symbols in the auric field, which lifts the soul and higher self to higher dimensions.

The final symbol, the sixth symbol, is the '*Fortification Symbol*'. This symbol decreases positive energy for protection. In other words, it hides a person's high vibration energy to prevent it being seen by undesirables. Good for use in crowded places, at a funeral, in a cinema, etc, where the glowing white of the individual concerned would be very visible amidst the heavier energies, and it prevents attack by energy vampires.

The Goddess of Light Reiki opens you to invoke the power you need to complete your work on earth, the work you yourself chose to do before you entered this incarnation. With the Goddesses of Light around you, you have control of your life and you have the power to manifest what you need to reach fulfilment and true happiness.

CHAPTER 17

LEMURIAN CRYSTAL REIKI

LEMURIAN CRYSTAL REIKI works with the crystal energy of the earth to balance, re-align and heal the physical and spiritual body with the power of love. Lemurian Reiki is a powerful light detoxant which transforms negative particles. Since 2012, many crystals have been activated within the earth, and this awakened energy will assist healers who have been attuned to Lemurian Reiki. With the Lemurian Reiki attunement, you will be initiated into the Lemurian consciousness.

The ancient lost civilization of Lemuria existed before and during the time of Atlantis. Lemuria was located in the Southern Pacific, between North America, Asia and Australia. The people of Lemuria came from another universe, so were both highly evolved and very Spiritual. They were explorers, searching for spiritual knowledge and for habitable planets on which to settle. Some of them settled on earth, populating the areas which were linked to different planets and star constellations. From here, they were able to communicate with their home world through the use of crystals, which emitted a beam of energy into space and was picked up by other crystals. The Lemurian lineage is the Aborigine culture, one of the present holders of the sacred secrets of the earth.

Approximately 14,000 years ago, both Atlantis and Lemuria were thriving, but they evolved separately and did not have contact with each other. Like the Atlanteans, the Lemurians were far in advance of us in technology, psychic powers, healing methods, mind control and telepathy. They were very tall, about seven feet, with slim bodies, similar to the Pleiadians. As they were fifth-dimensional beings, more etherical than physical, their aura was strong, which made their bodies look translucent. Their hair was white or blonde with their facial features and skin albino-like. They had striking purple-blue eyes with large pupils and white or blonde eyelashes. They were a race of people strongly connected to Source and Nature, much more so than we are today. They were not as strongly connected to their bodies as we are, as they vibrated at a much higher frequency level than we do. This meant they could levitate out of their physical bodies to be as one with animals, plants and their environment. Our Lemurian spirit guides have been waiting for us heavy vibrational humans to raise our frequency in the 2012 attunement process of the earth, in order to merge their energy with ours. They have been evaluating our Spiritual progress, and have selected each one of us for our eagerness to learn Spiritual knowledge and for our love of crystals.

The Lemurians, being highly evolved beings, were peaceful and loving. They communicated by telepathic thought process and emotions. Unlike the Atlanteans, the Lemurians did not mix with others not of their kind, remaining solitary and isolated.

The Lemurian Spiritual Elders were aware that a dramatic disaster was about to happen in the future on earth. This turned out to be the great flood, which resulted in Atlantis sinking beneath the ocean. The Lemurians prepared for this great cataclysm by storing information in crystals, which they buried deep within the earth, with their own vibration, and which they programmed to re-awaken after the 2012 attunements of the earth. The crystals they chose were slender pointed and from the quartz family, usually the clear quartz. These crystals we now call Lemurian Seed Crystals. A Lemurian seed crystal has a different vibration frequency to the normal master quartz. These crystals have amazing energy with which to meditate, so you can download subconsciously their Lemurian library of secrets.

The Lemurian Spiritual leaders were experts in understanding not only the amazing healing energy and powers of crystals, but also the ability to store etheric information. The Spiritual Elders were able to meditate with the crystals so information from the elders' minds could be stored for future generations within the energy of the crystal. By delaying the awakening or re-activation of the crystals, the Lemurian Spiritual Elders safe-guarded their information from falling into the wrong hands, by knowing that Lightworkers would be ready. As a result, at this present time, ancient knowledge is being released to Lightworkers all over the planet.

Knowledge was also stored in human DNA, with many people around the world completely unaware of the knowledge they stored. Now, however, since the Earth's spiritual attunements in 2012, more and more people are becoming aware and opening up to new Spiritual experiences and phenomena, with their hidden psychic gifts revealed, and the realisation and remembering of codes and knowledge long embedded in their soul. This Lemurian knowledge is about sacred geometry and the specific gridding of crystals to create vortexes to connect back to Source. The beings of Lemuria knew it was very important that the information and knowledge they held be saved, for otherwise the sacred teachings would have been lost forever.

Since 2012, the buried crystals and the coded DNA have been awakening, opening up, not just memories of Lightworkers and advanced Spiritual people, but wakening up also new and powerful vortexes to other solar systems and the higher realms. These vortexes will enable souls to by-pass the seven etheric Spiritual layers of the earth and travel directly to Source. In the past, Spiritual people have had to learn and evolve in their dream work by gaining knowledge and experience on each level. Amongst us now are numerous people who have been closed down Spiritually, so they have no idea they are guardians of Lemurian secrets within their DNA. These people have blended in and until now were not interested in matters Spiritual, but now suddenly find themselves awakened and rapidly becoming natural powerful healers and mature Spiritual beings. It is all part of the Divine plan for earth and the entire cosmos. Everything is as it should be, and all will manifest in Divine Timing.

Lemurian Spiritual Elders have given humans a special gift by our chance to evolve much more quickly with the help of crystals. Lemurian Spiritual souls who have been preparing to be spirit guides will have been summoned by the re-activation of the crystals to be ready after Lemurian Reiki attunement.

The Lemurians built the underground city of Telos, under Mount Shasta, in California, as a safe refuge from the impending disaster. Today, Mount Shasta is one of the major portals through which higher beings of Light, enter and exit our earthly vibrational plane.

Lord Melchizedek is the Ascended Master associated with Lemuria, the energy being channelled directly from him. Lord Melchizedek's name translated means 'My King is Righteousness'. In his incarnations on earth, he was a king and a high priest and was also known as 'The Prince of Peace'. Lord Melchizedek is a powerful being who oversees the Ascension process and the development of all beings in this universe. He is a gentle, father figure, whom many people have met in their dreams, believing him to be Source. He supports all beings, angels, spirit guides and human souls, and offers advice to all the Ascended Masters and Archangels.

Lord Melchizedek is a very old soul, so when Lemuria was created, he was relatively young, but even then, Spiritually very mature. Melchizedek incarnated in spirit form to the Lemurian priests and priestesses to give them Spiritual teachings. They sought his guidance on Spiritual matters and earthly issues, especially when they knew about the great flood. Today, Lord Melchizedek is continuing his work as the right hand 'Man' of God, in preparing the coming of new Ascended Masters on earth and on other dimensions.

When you are attuned to Lemurian Reiki, you may experience feelings of warmth, coolness and pulsing, as the Lemurian energy is charged through your body. The pulsing will be the energy opening and closing your chakras so they can be aligned and balanced in readiness for you to channel Lemurian Reiki. Any suppressed memories or Spiritual gifts will be awakened in your DNA. This attunement will feel different from other attunements you may have had previously, as this will awaken all the cells in your body and energise the water modules in your physical body. This sensation may feel strange, but to many of you it will feel normal, as you were probably once a priest or priestess of Lemuria, over thousands of years ago.

The Lemurians placed crystals to activate earth's crystal grids to connect to other planets after the 2012 alignment. So now, Lemurian Crystal Reiki also enables healers to invoke universal energy of many stars, planets and constellations, including Orion, Jupiter and Pluto. This awakened energy helps all Lightworkers to feel at home with the rebirth of our earth's enlightenment frequency. Lemurian Crystal Reiki has come as an advanced energy to assist Ascended Masters and Lightworkers living on earth now. Even though many civilizations have long gone since the Lemurians were alive, there will still be spirits and energies belonging to that race of people here on earth. These spirits are Light beings. Some we know are the Orions who are good healers; those from Neptune who are teacher guides, and the reptilians who are protectors. But there are many more species from the universal Heavens whom we have not yet met, nor do we even yet know of their existence.

The energy of Lemurian Reiki symbols is based around love, so there is not a Lemurian Reiki symbol for protection. Love in itself is a defense against any lower energies as they are repelled and unable to function against the Lemurian energy.

There are five symbols in Lemurian Crystal Reiki.

The first symbol is the '*Universal Love Symbol*'. It goes without saying that everyone needs to be loved by others, but more importantly, to feel love for themselves. Many people find it hard to give themselves love; they open their heart to others and are selfless. This symbol releases a person from always feeling they have an obligation to heal everyone. It helps to release oaths and promises, for example, many Spiritual people pick partners who are of lower energy, in the hope that they can heal them. This symbol helps 'under-dogs' to regain respect and love for themselves and not be a life victim.

The second symbol, the '*Freedom of Being Symbol*', is used for a person who is afraid of who they are, or those who have lost confidence in themselves. It increases self-belief in life purpose and gives confidence in decision making, with the energy of the symbol deflecting psychic attacks. It helps those with issues relating to depression, guilt, rejection, redundancy, life changes and betrayal.

The third symbol, the '*Crystal Activation Key Symbol*', re-energises, cleanses and re-programmes crystals to any purpose. It should be used regularly to charge and refresh the energy of your crystals.

The fourth symbol, the '*Lemurian Portal Key Symbol*', is not for healing, but for use only to help with meditation and not for clients, but for the practitioner. This energy enables you to travel to other dimensions which includes other planets and the seven etheric layers in the higher realms. This portal key will activate your soul energy to open its crown chakra vortex to a higher frequency so you can travel further and faster. You need to make sure you ground yourself strongly and protect yourself before using this symbol.

The final symbol, the '*Lemurian Master Symbol*', increases your Lemurian Reiki energy. With many clients, you may not feel you need to increase your energy unless they are very Spiritually mature. It is useful to increase the energy for the crystals in your therapy room just before a healing session.

The new practitioner is also given the '*Lord Melchizedek Seal*', which dates back to the time of the Old Testament as a symbol of God Himself. Many religions have used this symbol to express their belief in Christianity and have worn it in jewellery to protect them. Nowadays, Spiritual and New Age people use this symbol in meditation to bring in the Divine Light from Source. The various components of the symbol represent eternity and the sun, which is the source of all light; new beginnings; the highest order of the Melchizedek Priesthood; earth; mortal life, and the number 8, which is the infinity symbol.

As a practitioner of Lemurian Crystal Reiki, the Lemurian Elders will continue to light your way with amazing love. Be proud of who you are, how far you have come, and what you have achieved.

Never ever underestimate the power of crystals. They were the main source of energy and power for ancient civilizations. Today, quartz crystals are used in watches and computers. Your crystals are willing to work with you in sharing their energy, helping you to enjoy the life you live. Your Lemurian Crystal Reiki course also includes showing you how to build crystal grids to call in the energy from the stars and other planets in the galaxy.

CHAPTER 18

OKUNA REIKI

OKUNA REIKI has been channelled by Mirta Larrea from Argentina, a Usui Reiki Master and Teacher since 1998. It has its origins in ancient Lemuria and Atlantis. It channels energy from the stars and brings peace and bliss for everyone. Many thousands of years have passed since the Lemurian and Atlantean civilizations, but we can access these again now, at the start of the Aquarian Age, through the symbols involved in Okuna Reiki, as the pure energy of Lemuria and Atlantis is returning.

Lemuria was a continent in the Southern Hemisphere. Atlantis was a huge land mass linking Africa and Europe with North and South America. Today, the Canary Islands, the Azores and Bermuda, are all remaining parts of the continent of Atlantis. Almost everyone on earth has had an incarnation in Atlantis.

The Lemurians preceded the Atlanteans. They were fifth-dimensional beings, ethereal, without physical form as we understand it; androgynous; complete in themselves, reproducing by conscious will and energy transference.

Atlantis was a Divine experiment to see if humans could live in a physical body and still retain their connection with Source. They were gifted with remarkable psychic and Spiritual abilities, far beyond our present human understanding or comprehension. During the Golden Age of Atlantis, which lasted for over 1,500 years, the Spiritual energy on planet earth was the highest it has ever been. It was called Golden Atlantis because the energy was so pure and of such high vibration that it emitted a golden glow colour from the aura of each person, and also from the land.

The Atlanteans were far in advance of us in healing, using energetic vibrations, telepathy, clairvoyancy, clairaudiency, tele-porting, stones and crystals, magnets, mathematics, astrology, and their awesome psychic abilities. Their technology was so far ahead of ours that we cannot even begin to imagine what it was like. Their main source of energy was through huge crystals which they programmed to work for them. A crystal was the focal point of each temple. All the crystals were connected to each other, and also connected to the magnificent generator crystal in the temple of Poseidon. They built stone circles with a pre-determined link to a star, through which they could draw in wisdom and knowledge from the galaxies. They lived totally in the moment, aware only of the present, joyously celebrating all that they had, with no concept of tomorrow. They understood everything about energy and vibrational and dimensional differences.

Over time, however, the human ego began to take over, and the Atlantis Civilization fell prey to greed, lust for power and desire for control. These humans with free will deviated further from their Source and deeper into matter, materialism and self-destruction. As a result of the separation from Source, Atlantis was sunk beneath the ocean, around where the infamous Bermuda Triangle is now considered to be. The huge crystal which acted as their power generator, in their Temple of Poseidon, sank with everything else and it is the energy from that crystal, now being re-activated with the recent magnetic shifts in the entire cosmos, that has been causing planes and ships to disappear in mysterious circumstances. Scientists continue to look in all the wrong places for the answer, simply because they are looking for a rational explanation, instead of accepting that there are numerous dimensions and vibrational frequencies all around us, invisible to our limited human vision, and far beyond our limited human conception.

Before Atlantis sank, the original high priests and priestesses, who later became mythical Gods in Egypt and Greece, each led one of the twelve tribes to a new location, so the genetic wisdom of Atlantis on earth was maintained. Here, they interbred with the local people, sharing their awesome gifts and knowledge with them. These twelve tribes joined the Incas and Aztecs in South America; the Babylonians; the Egyptians; the Innuit; the Mayans; the Kahunas in Hawaii; the Mesopotamians; the Maori in New Zealand; the Greeks and the Tibetans. Today it is these cultures that still hold the keys to Spirituality here on earth. And it was to these cultures the Atlanteans travelled, and it was these cultures the Atlanteans seeded.

Tens of thousands of years ago, indigenous cultures realised they could commune with the unseen Spiritual realms to ask for healing, weather changes, abundance of food and other needs. The shaman, or medicine person, whether alone or with a group, gained Spiritual, intuitive guidance through various means, such as repetitive chanting, percussion sounds, hallucinogenic plant medicine, ritual dance, and the induction of hypnotic trance. What exactly was happening here? Was this all some weird, spooky process by which evil spirits were conjured up for some particular purpose, a bit like the witches in Shakespeare's "Macbeth"? Not at all! These were just diverse ways by which these indigenous peoples managed to raise their vibrational level in order to communicate with the higher realm, to whom they knew they were connected. The Native American Indians, for example, regularly performed the rain dance, a combination of percussion sounds with the rain stick, and ritual dance movements, to ask for rain for the nourishment of Mother Earth, and they regularly smoked the pipe, to enable them to reach a higher vibrational level in order to attain spiritual wisdom and knowledge. These traditional, tribal cultures, continue to operate in various regions of the globe, honouring the natural cycles of the sun, the moon and the seasons.

Today in Bali, young men continue to perform ritual dances in order to induce a trance; when they can pierce their body with a knife and not feel it or not shed any blood, then they know they have reached the required state of trance.

Beings from Lemuria and Atlantis are amongst us today, but of course on a much higher vibration, to help planet earth evolve. We cannot evolve individually. We are all united, and we must all evolve collectively. So the Atlanteans and Lemurians are here to help us, and in helping us, they are also increasing their own evolutionary rate.

Okuna Reiki is based on the ancient Lemurian and Atlantean healing methods, using the ancient sacred symbols of Lemuria and Atlantis. It brings a deep cleansing of long-held blockages and negative patterns, solving ancestral blockages, leaving you with a feeling of freedom and relief, giving you back energy and happiness, filling you with cosmic love, coming from the planets and the stars.

Okuna Reiki raises the vibration, changing our energy from the third to the fourth dimension, and healing physically, mentally, emotionally and spiritually.

There are 6 symbols, all based on circles and triangles, and all connected to a particular crystal.

Firsly, the '*Ekahem Symbol*', which is used to help Mother Earth, with the clear quartz crystal.

Secondly, the '*Okuhey Symbol*', which is used for protection, using the tourmaline quartz.

Thirdly, the '*Okuyo Symbol*', which is used for transmutation, with the amethyst crystal.

Fourthly, the '*Elahem Symbol*', which is used for manifestation, to bring positive changes in your life, helping you to achieve your goals, and to dissolve negative patterns. The crystal here is the tiger's eye.

Fifthly, the '*Okyoho Symbol*', is used for creativity, to heal Illness, especially rheumatism, and can also be applied to places where earthquakes or other natural disasters have occurred. The crystal used with this symbol is orange calcite.

And finally, the' *Eakah Symbol* ', which is used to bring in unconditional love, universal love, and can be applied to the planets and areas here on earth where there is war. The crystal here is pink tourmaline.

Okuna Reiki is a strong, powerful healing system, based on the higher dimensional energy frequencies of ancient Lemuria and Atlantis, using the same symbols, the same crystals, and bringing a sense of peace, well-being and tranquillity to all.

CHAPTER 19

ARCHANGEL ASCENDED MASTER REIKI

Archangel Ascended Master Reiki: Since 2012 and the upliftment of the earth's vibration, new advanced energy is now being channelled to Lightworkers on earth. Never before has the angelic realm been able to descend close to the physical energy of the earth for long periods of time. Now for the first time, many Ascended Masters and Archangels are able to combine and unite their energy to assist Reiki masters. Archangel Metatron and Ascended Master Sananda (Jesus) unite their energy in this extraordinary healing modality using the new Ascension Ray called the Opal Healing Ray. The Opal Ray camouflages Lightworkers from dark beings especially off-planet saboteurs that are trying to prevent Ascension.

Archangels are the angels which have evolved into advanced light beings over many thousands of years. Their role is to oversee the angels who watch over human beings and to help Source. Archangels are the highest ranking angels in heaven, and they do their work both in the heavenly dimension and in the earthly one

There are two exceptional Archangels who are different from the others and they are the Archangels Metatron and Sandalphon, because they were once human. One of these, Metatron, has been chosen to work with the Opal Ray and help healers attune to its energy.

Ascended Masters are souls that have been many times in human bodies through various life experiences. Their souls will have learned good and bad ways through which they have evolved into a wise being. Ascended Masters have received many initiations/attunements in the Higher Realms. They now each hold positions of great responsibility, overseeing the earth and its growth, or they work on a cosmic level. They sometimes change their positions and gain 'promotion' by their service and help to humanity.

New Ascended Masters are evolving all the time. For the first time on earth there will be Ascended Master in human form walking amongst us, and this has only been made possible since the earth's attunements in 2012.

Every person is evolving into an Ascended Master, with some taking longer than others to learn life's lessons.

For centuries Archangels have watched over mankind but until now they have remained in the upper etheric levels of heaven. The current energy of earth has enabled angelic souls to adapt into a solid form by them becoming human. There are more angel people than ever before with some Lemurian and Atlantean souls returning to a human form.

When a healer is attuned to the Archangels they will have nightly tuition in their dreams from an Archangel. The healer will often have no memory of what has happened, but will develop inner feelings of confidence or wisdom.

Metatron is often the first Archangel to counsel lightworkers attuned to Archangel Reiki, because of his experience of being human when he was on earth as the prophet Enoch. He is able to advise the lightworker on how to see things from a human perspective. He is very good at solving problems on a personal basis, especially when the person is worried about solving an analytical problem.

Metatron is the Chancellor of Heaven and works closely with the Lords of Karma and is the keeper of the heavenly archives. Metatron for a long time has been working with the Lords of Karma and Ascended Masters so it was a natural progression that he suggested the Ascended Master Opal Healing Ray. Metatron was and is the ideal choice to initiate healers with the help of Sananda to the Archangel Ascended Master Reiki.

Archangel Ascended Master healing is powerful as it will change and adapt to the needs of the individual. This energy seems to have a 'mind of its own' and is rarely felt the same. Archangel Ascended Master energy changes its frequency to respond to what is injured or blocked. It is very versatile in that it can work on the soul and the mind at the same time as working on the physical body.

Metatron works with his symbols to channel energy down a healer's crown chakra vortex. He then spins and pulsates his symbols to create a powerul healing beam. His healing is sent in the form of the vibration of those sacred geometric shapes entering your system at your crown chakra and flowing through all chakras for perfect balance.

Ascended Master Sananda was formally known as Jesus. Sananda is a very humble and private Light being who often helps healers in the 'back-ground'. He works to help all mankind, especially children who have chosen spiritual parents. Sananda helps many lightworkers in their dreams by giving them advice and counselling them on human and spiritual problems. He is wise and a very good listener. Sananda is one of the members of the High Council and of the Universal Lords. He represents earth on many Universal matters and has an understanding of many Light beings of other worlds.

Sananda's previous lives include Adam, Jeshua, Joshua, Elijah and Joseph of Egypt. Until recently, he was working with Archangel Uriel to bring peace, brotherhood, service and freedom to people. This is another reason why Sananda was chosen to help Metatron with his work helping Uriel.

Until recently, Sananda was always accompanied by his Mother Mary and Mary Magdalene. Since the energy change in 2012 both Marys have developed their own roles and responsibilities separate to Sananda.

Mary Magdalene is currently helping new souls before they come to earth for the first time.

Mother Mary who was the human mother of Sananda when he lived as Jesus, is a powerful, beautiful Ascended Master of great love, wisdom and compassion. She often works with Quan Yin in helping women who have lost confidence to empower themselves. In her previous life she was Goddess Isis. She is now the twin flame, the celestial wife of Archangel Raphael.

Mother Mary's husband and Sananda's father, Saint Joseph, reincarnated as

Saint Germaine. Sananda and his human family still have an important role within the Higher Realms.

The Opal Ray is a universal translucent vibrational ray which combines the Ascended Master and Archangel Energy. It has two main aims. One is to hide the light worker or their client from harmful off-planet beings, and two is to create confusion as the Opal Ray changes frequency continually. Metatron uses the Opal Ray to create a spiral vortex to encase the negative being so they are secured in order to be transported safely away from harm. The Opal Ray does not 'protect', but hides the person from harmful influences, the Golden protective energy must still be used.

After your attunement to the Archangel Ascended Master energy, this Opal Ray will be accessible to you whenever you may need it.

Archangel Metatron is associated with sacred geometric shapes and protective grids.

The first symbol is the Metatron Star also known as the Merkaba Star, a combination of a series of triangles, very powerful in a room to keep the Divine light energy strong.

The second symbol is the Flower of Life, one of the oldest symbols known to man, and composed of many evenly spaced and overlapping circles, arranged in a way to form the flower-like pattern.

The third symbol is Metatron's Cube, representing how God has made shapes to fit together throughout creation, the way people's bodies and souls fit together.

The fourth symbol is Archangel Michael's protection symbol, a circle within a triangle.

The fifth symbol is the Shanti, similar to the Dai Ko Myo master Reiki symbol, but has the additional energy of the Archangel Reiki.

After your attunement, just allow the guidance of the Archangels and Ascended Masters to lead you on your chosen path to happiness and love!

CHAPTER 20

GOLDEN RAINBOW RAY REIKI

GOLDEN RAINBOW RAY REIKI: All light beings use colour in many ways when they are working. The Ascended Masters work with a colour ray for a specific purpose and role. This Golden Rainbow Ray Reiki is an attunement to the Highest Ray which is the Golden Ray. The Golden Ray will help you to sense and detect colour changes in your environment, in yourself and of course in your client. The Ascended Masters are not the only light beings that use the Rays. The Archangels also have the ability to channel colour in healing and protection. With each colour Ray there are symbols which help to intensify the vibrational colour energy.

Colour is important in our lives, determining our moods and feelings.

This course teaches you how all the different colours each have a different effect and how they are all used for different purposes.

Colour helps healing because each colour has its own vibration and so it can encourage an area of the body to absorb the colour to aid healing. If the colour is darker but the same shade as the chakra, it can slow down the vibration of the energy of the chakras. If a chakra is closed and sluggish, for example the throat, then a lighter shade of blue will help to increase the vibrational energy around that area.

Using colour during a Reiki healing session will help the aura vibrate using the natural colour energy within the auric field to stabilise itself and become healthy. The colours will naturally align the aura so that any holes or cracks will be healed.

Having a weak auric field is unhealthy, not just in a physical sense where we feel tired, but in a spiritual sense where we are vulnerable to negative spirits or energies. After your attunement, you will be able to bring in the Golden Rainbow Ray which will help to restore energy within your aura and in doing so will help all of your energy, mentally, physically and spiritually.

Gold is the strongest protective energy and a being who is able to channel this energy can use the gold to increase their soul energy to help repel negative beings. Gold is a shield energy, it does not convert negative energy but creates a barrier. The Golden Rainbow Ray cannot prevent you from feeling sad, angry or upset, but it can help you to clear yourself by you being unsavoury to other lower beings.

The Golden Rainbow Ray contains all the colours of the spectrum so you can invoke a particular colour within the Golden Ray itself, for example pink within the Golden Ray to help the heart chakra.

This course teaches you about the different colour rays of the various Archangels and Ascended Masters and their purposes. You also learn about the Rainbow Bridge.

The symbols coincide with the chakras.

The Soul Star is gold, and helps you to connect to your Higher Self, your guardian angel and the Lords of Karma.

The Crown is indigo/violet and helps spiritually closed people to open up, increases spiritual awareness and balances human and spiritual thought.

The Third Eye is purple and helps you to see spiritual energy using physical human sight.

The Throat is blue and is really effective in opening or closing the throat chakra.

The Heart is green with a rose pink centre. If a person is vulnerable and too eager for love then the heart chakra is too open so it will need more green. If a person is feeling hurt and angry with love, then the heart chakra is too closed and will need more pink.

The Ascension colour is silver and prepares us for Ascension and for the completion of our life's purpose.

The Solar Plexus colour is yellow and this symbol unlocks the buried emotional secrets of the solar plexus, which all of us carry.

The Sacral/ Base chakra ia red/orange and this symbol helps to ground and open up kundalini energy.

The Earth Star chakra is brown/sage green and this symbol is used at the end of a healing session to bring down the energy to connect to earth and stabilise the client's auric field.

Using the Golden Rainbow Ray daily will cleanse and energise your energy. Use the colour of your clothes to create energy within your auric field and to lift your vibration. Colours have their own unique energy, so allow them to enhance all aspects of your life!

Have a colourful life!

CHAPTER 21:

GOLDEN CHALICE REIKI

Golden Chalice Reiki vibrational energy is a Universal energy which originated from the combined Spiritual energies of Venus and Saturn. The Great White Brotherhood and the Universal Lords have been recruiting Spiritual souls to be guardians of the Golden Chalice energy. These souls consist of both earth souls in solid body and light beings in the Higher Realms.

The Great White Brotherhood is made up of all the Ascended Masters and is responsible for teaching the lightworkers on earth; some of them are also members of the Lords of Karma. Even though they are referred to as the Great White Brotherhood, this does not mean they are all male energy. The members also consist of female energy. Recently the Great White Brotherhood have new members who are still in a physical body on earth. This has occurred due to the earth's recent Attunement in 2012. So this may mean that a female energy within the Brotherhood is a man as an earth soul and a male member of the Brotherhood could be a woman in a physical body.

The Universal Lords are spiritual beings from all planets who meet to discuss anything that affects the balance of power within the Universe. Earth's representative is Ascended Master Sananda (Jesus). The Universal Lords ensure all planets and the etheric heavenly realms are not overpowered by any negative being. But they also understand the necessity of the dark side having a part to play in light beings' evolution.

The Universal Lords will instruct lightworkers on how to use the power of the Golden Chalice for healing and protection. They will do this while the lightworker is awake and alert, leaving the dream experiences to the White Brotherhood. They teach healers how to expand their energy to absorb more of the power of the Golden Chalice. Healers may find themselves 'growing' by becoming taller with the crown chakra being pulled upwards. It is a lovely feeling which makes the healer feel they are at one with the Golden Chalice energy.

Golden Chalice Spirit Guides are selected by the Great White Brotherhood (Earth) and the Universal Lords (Galactic). The guides are chosen for their steadfast loyalty in protecting the Golden Chalice energy, even to the 'death'. If a lightworker becomes egoistic or disrespectful of the power of the Golden Chalice these guides have been ordered to withdraw the Golden Chalice. These Guides' only concern is that the energy of the Golden Chalice is used with love and for the good of all.

The Great White Brotherhood selects only loving combat soldiers who are quite often one of the noble knights of the Knights Templar or Saint John. Your guides join you approximately 2 to 3 weeks prior to your Attunement, and you may have restless nights and feel tired in the mornings. Your Golden Chalice Guides will be able to clear you of all negative beings and negative energy, so long as you are respectful. When you are cleared and cleansed you will feel a shiver of Golden Chalice energy down your spine and across your shoulders. This shiver is a signal from your Golden Chalice Guides that all is well and you are cleared. Golden Chalice Guides will instruct their lightworker healer how to channel the Golden Chalice energy to use in psychic defence, healing and meditation.

Dragons and unicorns assist Golden Chalice Knights in combat against the underworld, forming an immensely powerful partnership against all the dark forces.

Healing with Golden Chalice Reiki increases confidence, self-belief, self-worth and faith in Universal intervention. Golden Chalice Reiki works on the solar plexus, heart and ascension chakras. Healing penetrates deep into soul level to increase hope, faith, abundance and reward.

The symbols for Golden Chalice Reiki are Justice; Trust; Harmony and Balance; Insight; Faith and Hope.

Golden Chalice Reiki will enrich your life and others you meet. The wisdom of your Chalice Guides will teach you to have positive thoughts and to live each day as a gift. Respect and love yourself so others will cherish their time with you. You are special because you have been chosen to carry the Golden Chalice power. Use this power wisely so you enrich your life with love, abundance and happiness.

CHAPTER 22:

MARY MAGDALENE REIKI

Mary Magdalene Reiki is the most recent of the newer healing modalities to be channeled. Mary Magdalene's energy is very different from the energy of Mother Mary in that while Mother Mary energy is very calm and soothing, Mary Magdalene's energy is very up-beat, very feisty, and almost urgent, as if she is saying: 'Let's go! Let's do this! Come on!' Almost as if she is rallying the troops for a great mission!

Mary Magdalene Reiki has been channeled by Alessandra Rossin, Reiki Master teacher, Bienestar Ibiza, Santa Eulalia, Ibiza. It is a healing technique that has been born from the merging of many seminars made in the last 20 years. Very simple and uncomplicated, Mary Magdalene Reiki is a truly beautiful healing modality.

Mary Magdalene's time has indeed come! Her story is being made known across the world, her real role in the life of Jesus is being revealed bit by bit. She was NOT the prostitute, the sinner or the woman possessed by seven demons that the early Christian Church fathers made her out to be. She was the Spiritual partner of Jesus, his Spiritual equal and the one most capable of carrying on his teachings after the Crucifixion. She was the '*apostle to the apostles*', the one who explained Jesus' teachings to the others, who very often failed to get the meaning of his words.

She was a victim of her times, a woman in a male-dominated, patriarchal society, holding her own against all the odds, castigated by a misogynistic so-called Christian Church simply because she was a woman, and a powerful woman. She was not to be tolerated simply because she was the sexual partner of their celibate, divine, supernatural son of a supernatural god, the person they named as Jesus, but known to the disciples and to Mary Magdalene as Yeshua.

Mary Magdalene represents the Divine Feminine, in perfect balance with Yeshua, the perfect balance between the feminine energy and the masculine energy.

Our world is so troubled right now because the masculine energy has been allowed to dominate for the last 2,000 years and more, creating an unbalanced world where war, aggression and violence are constant.

It is now time to restore the feminine energy to equal status with the masculine energy, each complementing the other, bringing a new glorious dawn, a new age, where people live in peace and harmony in the totality of Father/Mother God, and not in the limitation of a punishing, vengeful male God somewhere up in the clouds beyond the earth plane.

It is time for each of us to balance the feminine and masculine within each of us, reflecting the balance of Father/Mother God throughout all creation, and to experience the joy and unlimited potentiality of living in the fullness of the totality rather than existing in the limitation of either just one or the other.

There is only one symbol in Mary Magdalene Reiki and that is the Cross. The vertical line in the cross represents the masculine and the horizontal line represents the feminine. They are both equal.

Mary Magdalene's colours are crimson and gold, and her flower is the rose. We see the word ROSE encapsulated in the anagram with the word EROS, the Greek god of sexual attraction. From ancient times, the rose has been depicted at the heart of a cross. A deep and profound mystery lies in the image of the rose that blooms at the heart of the cross. The rose is fathomless in its beauty and in its meaning. A flower of great, mesmerising beauty and intoxicating fragrance, it is the symbol of Mary Magdalene.

CHAPTER 23:

PYRAMID OF ISIS REIKI

Pyramid of Isis Reiki is associated with Egypt and incorporates ancient and new Reiki healing power with the addition of working with pyramids. Pyramid of Isis Reiki is a combination of the Egyptian attunements of Isis Moon, Sekham Seichem, Golden Ankh, Ra Sheeba (Golden Snake), Pyramid Gaza, Sacred Geometry and Golden Triangle Reiki.

Goddess Isis is one of the Goddesses of Light who are guardians of the Light Ray. Isis works with the other Goddesses of Light, Amerissis, Theia, Artemis and Athena. The Light Goddesses empower female energy in male and female lightworkers.

Goddess Isis was worshipped in ancient times and modern day Wiccan as the mother Goddess, also as the patroness of nature and magic. Isis is also known as the protector of the dead and Goddess of children. Some people refer to Goddess Isis as the protector of Love. Her name Isis means 'throne', her headress was a throne and as such, she represented the Pharaoh's power.

The other Reiki energies which collectively create the Pyramid of Isis Master Reiki are:

ISIS MOON: Working with Goddess Isis and the magnetic energy field of the moon. Harmonising female and male energy.

SEKHAM SEICHEM MASTER: Ancient Egyptian healing energy using similar symbols to traditional Dr. Usui Japanese Reiki.

GOLDEN ANKH: Ancient Egyptian healing energy helping healers meditate to a higher level using the Ankh energy to open spiritual portals.

GOLDEN TRIANGLE: Modern Reiki energy combining the Golden Ray energy with the geometric healing of triangles to shield and dissolve negative energy.

RA SHEEBA: A long forgotten Egyptian energy which was re-awakened in the 1980s to help healers open up healing vortexes throughout the world. Works directly on the chakras to lift out impurities using vortex movement. Helps healers with kundalini activation in the spine.

Attunement to Pyramid of Isis will activate geometric etheric energy within your aura. The energy will be intensified after your attunement to use your palm chakra healing for creating powerful etheric grids. These grids can be used to give additional power to your healing session as well as using the grid to create shields which protect against negative forces. Archangel Metatron creates etheric energy grids and now you too will have the ability to do the same.

Metatron instructs Goddess of Isis healers in their dreams on how to use the natural flow of the physical body using geometric shapes. One of these shapes is the triangle. The energy is channelled similar to crystal energy using laser waves pushing and pulling. Isis Reiki incorporates the Reiki with the natural flow of the meridian lines throughout the body to penetrate deeper on a cellular level.

Pyramid of Isis includes a joining of our energy to the Egyptian snake energy that has been worshipped in ancient Egypt by the Pharaohs. The Egyptian Priests and Priestesses invoked snake energy to give protection to sacred tombs, temples and themselves. Modern day healers often use the 'She' cobra to clear spaces with her ability to get dark creatures and take them to the White Light. She is a beautiful being who uses her ability to swallow dark matter and travel along vortexes to and from the White Light.

Reiki snake energy is a form of healing which focuses its frequency into healing energy vortex. It is very powerful, using sacred knowledge of the Egyptians, Atlanteans, Lemurians and the realms of the Dragons using vortexes. Snake energy healing is similar to spiral vortex energy of the Unicorns. The Snake Reiki works by lifting negativity out of the body upwards out of the chakras or along etheric cords and not through the chakras to the feet or head.

Isis Reiki also uses crystals, orgonites and copper for healing, as in ancient Egypt.

Symbols include: Triangle; the Uzu Symbol; Ahara; Isis; Akru; Tet; Infinity; Zara; Eeef T Chay; High-Low God; Connection Path; Seal of Isis and Sankak kei Symbol.

After your attunement, you will have the power to invoke the pyramid grid energy not just for healing but for creating a safe environment within your home and work.

Goddess Isis is a loving, wise and powerful ally to help you combat anything that makes you or others unhappy. Use her energy to connect you to the Golden Pyramid energy so you increase your psychic gifts in healing, protection and inner wisdom. On this course you will have been given the gift of Pyramid of Isis Reiki using Orgone energy and the powerful brass pyramid, possibly the strongest and most powerful healing to date.

CHAPTER 24:

REIKI GRAND MASTER

Becoming a Reiki Grand Master is an honour. Grand Master status is not a new energy but is an ancient vibration that is reserved for highly advanced spiritual people. Grand Master status is a privilege because there are not many people who have advanced to these levels, so you will be one of only a few on our planet, and certainly at the moment in the U.K. and Ireland.

The initiations you receive for Grand Master are levels 5 and 6, a positive powerful energy called Reiki-Laser Energy. The symbols are special and as such, should be reserved for Grand Masters and not for the general public.

One needs to be an active Reiki Master for at least 6 months prior to being initiated into these levels. Of course, a lot of people are already Grand Masters in their own right, or should I say their soul is. Grand Master initiation is ensuring the person's human body cells are vibrating at an increased rate to enable the person's soul to be active and not restricted by the body mass of the person.

Everyone has the potential to be a Grand Master and really it is up to the individual to feel they have reached a point in their life that they no longer want to be held back spiritually by human emotion and trauma. The Attunement process enables the higher self of the individual to have more influence on life's decisions which will then help the person fulfil their life's purpose. The higher self stores memories of all our soul's deeds, good and bad, which we have done as an angelic being prior to joining a human body and of course as a person in a physical form.

The requirement to become a Grand Master is not an egoistic issue or a big-headed attitude, but an inner knowing that the time is right. The requirements to become a Grand Master is not down to us making the decision, but more to our guides, our Ascended Masters and of course our higher self. In fact, Masters can be closed down because they become idealistic and big-headed. Even if any of us overstep the mark in the future, our Ascended Masters will intervene and ensure we are closed down, and then only reopened when the lesson of servitude has been learned. Even as Grand Masters, we must never give anyone the impression we are better than they are or we are more important, as after all, we are only the tools, the pencils, whereas our guides are the artists.

So what is a Reiki Grand Master?

A Reiki Grand Master is an individual who has progressed through to level 3, Master, and works with higher levels of vibration. All Reiki Masters have the potential to become 'Grand Masters' over time and with experience. As soon as we have our Masters attunement we are already being groomed for ascension. This means we are eligible to become 'Grand Masters' consciously or subconsciously, at whatever our area of expertise is.

Grand Master status is really our soul energy vibrating at an extremely high frequency which can penetrate into solid matter more easily than a Reiki practitioner. With our human bodies being made up of bone and solid matter, the increased vibration of a Grand Master is able to use the meridian lines to channel energy, for example, the ends of the fingers.

Some people have an inner knowing that they are 'stuck' spiritually which is preventing them from completing their life's purpose. This inner knowing is the person's higher self, who is urging the person to go as high as they can spiritually by increasing their vibration which then enables both the person and their higher self to go forward. It is almost as if the higher self can relax and allow natural spiritual forces to take control after the person has reached Grand Master frequency.

After your attunement to Grand Master level, you will become more complacent and accepting with life's challenges. Your soul will feel more relaxed, happy and content, with an inner feeling you have achieved something. Your inner feeling will be more intuitive with gut feelings and sensing things before they happen.

Grand Master energy can be channelled into the fingertips as well as the palm chakra of the attuned Grand Master healer. Because of this unique intense energy, you may find that when you do healing you will gently spread your fingers. With Reiki 1, 2, 3 and 4, the healing energy comes out of the palm chakras, and the healer has their hands cupped with their fingers closed.

The Grand Master is able to spread their fingers and the energy emits out of the tip of each finger, helping more than one person at a time. The laser energy beamed out will heal who or what is at the other end of the beam.

A Grand Master also has the ability to channel energy into their toes and feet. So wherever you go, you are healing the planet and the environment, simply by being there! How special is that?

There are 3 symbols, but out of respect for them I will not go into details here. I can however, let you know that they translate as the Wisdom Symbol; the Great Harmony symbol and the Great Separation symbol.

As Grand Masters, may you live your lives in the fullness of abundance, good fortune, health, happiness and filled with Love. Your path is before you, walk with your heads held high, respect others and shine your light so others can follow your lead.

CHAPTER 25

MAGNIFIED HEALING OF THE GOD MOST HIGH OF THE UNIVERSE

MAGNIFIED HEALING OF THE GOD MOST HIGH OF THE UNIVERSE was first introduced into the earth plane in 1983, channelled through Kathryn Anderson and Gizele King in Florida. The name for this healing modality was chosen by Quan Yin, who was responsible for bringing it forth to humanity. It is co-created and magnified with the Source of *All That Is*, hence the name.

Magnified Healing brings forth the healing energy from the highest possible vibration, and so is extremely powerful. Because of its extreme power, the student needs to be already attuned to some high vibrational forms of healing, and needs to have a full understanding of the chakras and aura, the Spiritual hierarchy, karma, Violet Fire and Flame, the Three-Fold Flame and the process of Ascension.

As above, so below. Just as we have a hierarchy in our world here on planet earth, so too, there is a highly structured hierarchy in the Spirit world, but unlike ours, it is not one of superiority, but of responsibility. Those who exist on the highest vibrational forms of energy are the '*Completed Ones'*; those who have triumphed over matter and physicality and who now sustain Divinity in their being. There are multiple levels of such beings, as there are multiple levels of Spiritual responsibilities, all devoted to manifesting and consolidating Divine Plan for the entire creation. Archangel Metatron is in charge of holding the whole of creation together, hence the Metatron Cube, a vast, exquisite network of cosmic equations, geometrical designs, mathematical equations, and sound and light

107

vibrations. Ascended Master Lord Melchizedek and Archangel Michael are also part of this High Command, part of this Spiritual Hierarchy, extending from the Completed Ones, right down through the different vibrational levels of Ascended Masters, Archangels, Angels and Spirit Guides. Ascended Master Lord Melchizedek is in charge of re-programming the consciousness of all humanity in order for us to collectively evolve as completed Spiritual beings.

The process that we call Ascension is simply the raising of our physical form to higher dimensions of Light, finally merging our energy with '*All That Is*'.

The Three-Fold Flame is the pink, blue and gold Christ Flame within the heart of each of us; the expression of the energies of the Father, the Son and the Holy Spirit; three-fold because it embodies the triple qualities of love, wisdom and power that each and every one of us needs to actualise and manifest within ourselves in order to gain Spiritual Enlightenment and completeness. The pink flume represents love coming from the heart; the blue flume represents power, coming from the throat chakra, and the gold flume represents wisdom coming from the third eye. It is on this powerful Three-Fold Flame that Magnified Healing is based.

The Violet Flame, first originating with Buddha, then passed to the care of Quan Yin, and now recently under the director-ship of Saint Germain, has been returned to humanity for the transmutation of all negativity, assisting us to further our evolution towards Enlightenment.

Karma is one of the seven Spiritual laws of the universe; the law of Cause and Effect. Man controls his own destiny, in that each of us reaps what we sow. Every action that is less than good must, and will be balanced by us either in this life-time or in future life-times. When we balance our karma, we no longer need to re-incarnate in a physical form. Karma trundles its way right down through history, subjecting not only the individual, but also the collective, as in families, countries, nations, races, governments. No one escapes; we are all subject to balancing our less-than-good deeds with our good deeds.

When we are initiated into the healing modality of Magnified Healing, we receive a Divine dispensation for all our accumulated negative karma. As well as that, part of the course involves teaching the process of keeping karma at bay, by regularly cleaning our slate, so to speak, and preventing it from piling up against us again.

Magnified Healing also teaches the process of increasing the flow of healing energy through the hands, flowing from the Dove, The Holy Spirit; aligning of our Spiritual centres, our chakras; clearing of our Light channel; sensitizing, awakening, rewiring and connecting our nervous system; scanning and healing the body, stimulating the calcium in the spine.

There is no attunement as such in Magnified Healing. Rather, the crown chakra, the heart chakra and the hands of the student are initiated with Magnified Healing Essence, a combination of flower essences which Kathryn and Gisele were guided to create by Quan Yin. Taking a drop of the Magnified Essence daily helps keep the emotional body centred, connected to the Divine. Using the essence daily in these very difficult and changing times helps support our inner alignment and stability, and helps us to sustain the prayers and healing that are so greatly needed for humanity at this time.

Magnified Healing is for use in self-healing, healing others and in absent healing.

This very special gift to the world of Magnified Healing will help manifest joy, freedom, abundance and perfection in our own lives and consequently in the lives of all others.

109

CHAPTER 26

RAHANNI CELESTIAL HEALING

RAHANNI CELESTIAL HEALING is a truly beautiful healing modality. To be a channel of Rahanni is a very humbling experience and a great privilege.

Rahanni means ' *Of One Heart* ', and this is a healing coming from the heart. 'Ra' relates to the name of the most powerful Ancient Egyptian Sun God, the Father of all creation, and also the mirror image of the Ascended Master Lord Melchizedek, overseer of the universe. 'Hanni' is the Hebrew girl's name meaning 'Favoured Grace'. The separation of man from Source is known as 'The Fall from Grace'. It is now the time for man to return to Source; for Grace to return to planet earth to assist in this great process towards Ascension. This is the most wonderful opportunity to connect with the higher beings of Light, to assist our planet in raising the Spiritual consciousness of all humanity; and to reconnect humanity to truth, love and compassion.

Rahanni, as a healing modality, is believed to have originated from Sirius, the Pleiades and Andromeda, star and galactic systems which are home to many advanced civilisations.

Those beings of Light in Andromeda, who know only Love, have been visiting earth for a very long time, studying mankind with a view to helping save our planet earth. The Pleiadians are a very advanced race, far superior to us in technology and Spirituality.

The Pleiades were a star system where higher energies coming to earth from other galaxies were stepped down before reaching the much lower and dense earth vibration. Even at present, many Star Children remain for a time on the Pleiades, a staging post before incarnation, in order to prepare for the slower frequencies here on planet earth. The Pleiadians are trying to guide the inhabitants of our earth along a renewed Spiritual path, towards Ascension.

Sirius is a star in the constellation Canis Major which can be seen from both the northern and southern hemispheres. It appears as the brightest star in the night sky and is also known as the '*Dog Star*'. Sirius is a very advanced civilisation and is home to a group of very highly evolved beings. It holds information about Spiritual technology, sacred geometry, science and higher mental understanding, and downloads it to those who are ready to visit its training establishment in the inner planes. Energies fron Sirius helped build the great temples and pyramids of Egypt, and they made a contract with Source to help bring in the 'Golden Age' to this planet. This starts with beaming in healing energies and methods never before known on earth. There are many of us here who have difficulty in accepting that healing Light is, indeed, being beamed from other dimensions of reality and from other star systems, but remember, we are all energy, all vibrating on different energy frequencies, as yet invisible to the human eye.

Rahanni vibrates on the pink ray of Light that corresponds with the heart centre, helping to release all fear-based thinking and negativity, and opening up humanity to truth, love and compassion, the three key concepts in Rahanni. The energy is beamed from the higher dimensions of Light by the Celestial Pink Angels, and helps all Lightworkers to connect to Lord Melchizedek and to Quan Yin, Goddess of Mercy and Compassion. It is also activated by the use of the *Six Pointed Star* plus the energies of the seven main Archangels,- Michael, Raphael, Chamuel, Gabriel, Jophiel, Zadkiel and Uriel. The Six Pointed Star is known as the '*Healing Star of Jesus*', and represents communion with the healing Light of Source. It is a star of Light, of brotherhood, and also the love that is held within every human heart.

The practitioner also invokes the energies of the Ascended Masters, Helios and Vesta on the gold and copper ray, and Phylos the Tibetan.

The simplicity of this healing art makes it accessible to everyone. To be able to tap into a healing Light that is pure love, truth and compassion, is truly wonderful. To help bring out that natural essence of pure unconditional love in others, adults and children alike, in order to give them a greater quality of life, is a most wonderful work.

There are three symbols in Rahanni, all coming from the heavenly dimensions of reality.

Frist, the '*Truth Symbol*', which represents the acceptance of self and the truth of who we are. This symbol recognises the need for a change in consciousness.

Second, the '*Love Symbol*', which recognises the love we hold in our heart. No matter how difficult our path has been, love has always been there.

Finally, the '*Compassion Symbol*', representing compassion for the world and for everyone in the world, at all times.

Rahanni Celestial Healing is not a therapy to come into just because you like the sound of it, or because you see it as a way to earn more money, but because you understand fully that the energy is coming from the heart. If you feel quite excited when you read about Rahanni, then maybe this is the time for you to bring this into your life.

Rahanni, however, cannot be combined with any other form of healing energy, such as Reiki, because of the different vibrations. So you need to decide at the start of a treatment whether you are going to give a Reiki treatment or a Rahanni treatment. Combining the two

Working With Spirit: A World of Healing

would not be of benefit to your client.

As long as you come from love, you cannot go wrong. You will be guided along your path in Divine Timing. Take the time to connect with your higher self, your own higher consciousness, and listen to the answer coming to you. Then you will know if Rahanni is for you!

CHAPTER 27

PSYCHIC SURGERY

PSYCHIC SURGERY is a technique that is part of the Kahuna Reiki. The word 'Kahuna' comes from Hawaii and means priest, master, expert and counsellor.

Psychic surgery is just that, surgery performed psychically. The client is at all times fully awake and fully clothed.

With this technique we can help at different levels: physical; emotional; mental or Spiritual. It is important to remember that this is not meant to replace medical help.

This technique can be taught on the third degree of Reiki. It can be combined with other kinds of Reiki, or used on its own. With this surgery, the practitioner goes to the blocked energy and removes it from the client. These blockages are the result of non-harmonic emotions such as envy, fear, hatred, jealousy, rancour, sadness etc.

During the surgery, a lot of emotions may be released, so tears or anger might surface.

113

The practitioner's hands do not touch the client. The illness is removed by the practitioner's extended fingers entering the client's aura and using pulling, scraping, scooping or massaging movements to extract whatever is found. Everything extracted is transmuted down to Mother Earth. If a cutting is required in order to remove the blockage, (psychically of course!) the wound will be sealed with amethyst or another suitable crystal.

Tera-Mai Reiki Seichem teaches an alternative variation of psychic surgery, whereby the practitioner removes the aura from the client, hands the aura over to the Angelic Kingdom for healing, and then restores the healed aura to the client again.

Psychic surgery, as a healing technique, requires no additional Attunement or symbols from the usual Reiki symbols. Once you have been attuned to Reiki One and Two, you are able to perform psychic surgery. The only difference is that you are actually going inside the person's aura and extracting the cause of the blockage or, as in Tera-Mai Reiki Seichem, removing the aura and handing it over to the Angels for healing.

Psychic surgery is simply an additional technique for use in Reiki healing. The course itself entails being shown how to use the visualisation techniques involved.

CHAPTER 28

TIBETAN SINGING BOWLS THERAPY

TIBETAN SINGING BOWLS THERAPY is not a healing modality that requires an attunement. It is a therapy, an ancient therapy, originating in Tibet, based on sound vibration and tonal resonations to move energy around the body. It is a beautiful healing treatment which induces a deep sense of relaxation, calmness and tranquillity.

Like most of the ancient traditions around the world, the origin of Tibetan bowls lies somewhere between legend and history. It is generally accepted that it all began during the 'Bon' Shamanic Dynasty, some 4,000 years before Christ. That's 2,000 years before Buddhism! So Tibetan singing bowls are actually pre-Buddha!

Musical instruments have always been used to honour the Gods in religious ceremonies and in pagan rituals. Tibetan singing bowls were used for all traditional shamanic rituals and they were manufactured in accordance with an old alchemist rule of seven, corresponding to the seven planets in the cosmos that were honoured as seven Gods: Gold- Sun; Silver- Moon; Mercury- Mercury; Iron- Mars; Tin- Jupiter; Lead- Saturn; Copper- Venus. Some believe that meteorite metal was added in some cases, meteorites being seen as a sign from the Gods, and then added to the other seven metals. The handmade art of the singing bowl is simple but very difficult to copy due to the alloy of these seven metals. It is still a secret craft, handed down through the generations from father to son, and this explains why they were originally only to be found in the Tibetan region. No one else has ever found the way to alloy the seven metals in the correct order and quantity to orchestrate their particular sounds and vibrations.

In 1969, with the Chinese invasion and take-over of Tibet, the Dalai-Lama fled to Northern India, followed by most of the Tibetan monks and Tibetan hand-craftsmen, who feared for their lives at the hands of the Chinese. They escaped across the mountains and found refuge mostly in Nepal and Bhutan. Most of their bowls were left in Tibet and subsequently destroyed by the Chinese, either because the Chinese invaders did not understand the significance of them, or just as part of the overall destruction and violence they perpetrated on the country. Just a few remained in some museums.

Today, Tibetan singing bowls are manufactured in Nepal by those Tibetan refugees and their descendants, and then exported all over the world.

However, nowadays we can find machine-manufactured bowls as well as the real hand-crafted Tibetan singing bowls. The machine-made bowls have only two or three metals incorporated into them, mostly bronze and nickel, unlike the handmade ones that are still composed of the seven original metals. The machine-manufactured bowls can be easily identified as they are a perfect round shape and with different colour shades.

Tibetan singing bowls come in all sizes, weights and colours. The smaller the bowl, the higher the sound it emits, the larger bowls emitting a much deeper sound and vibration. The largest bowls emit a sound like a huge gong, deep and very powerful. Everything in the universe including our human body, has a special and unique vibration. Time needs to be taken therefore when choosing your bowl, as you need to find one that resonates with your energy and one whose sound vibration matches your own.

The stick is equally as important as the bowl. The stick is used to create the sound through two specific movements: banging the side of the bowl and letting that sound peter out gradually; and ribbing, which means rubbing the stick right round the rib of the bowl in order to create a continuous sound. The traditional stick is made of wood, but you can also buy them now with one end wood and the other end in leather or hard cotton. The leather sticks are effective with the larger bowls, because they induce a deeper sound, without the typical scraping noise of the wooden side of the stick.

It is important to place your bowl on top of a cushion as a soft base, or you can hold it in the flat palm of your hand allowing it to sound and vibrate without distortion. The cushion, the same size as the base of the bowl, is usually included in the purchase of the bowl. You need to buy your bowl in a recommended outlet, a specialist outlet, where someone knowledgeable can help you choose the correct bowl for you, and not somewhere where they are just being sold as part of general merchandise, where the energy would not be at all suitable.

To maintain your bowl, you need to cleanse it sometimes in order to keep its energy pure. The traditional method is to use a lemon, cutting the lemon in half and rubbing the bowl in circles, one half of the lemon on the inside of the bowl, and the other half on the outside, until the lemon has taken on a green rust colour. Then the bowl needs to be rinsed with water to remove any residual lemon, and then dried. If you feel that your bowl needs a more thorough cleansing, maybe because you have been using it on other people, and it has therefore gathered up negative energy, then cleanse it with sage or incense sticks, or you can even Reiki it if you are attuned into Reiki.

Tibetan singing bowls are used to clear and refresh the aura and to cleanse and balance the chakras.

To clear the aura, simply take the bowl in your hand and place it in front of your third eye. Take a deep breath and concentrate on your bowl in order to connect with it and get the energy flowing easily. Bang it once to start the session, and then move it round your body within your aura, repeating the banging several times, until you feel your aura completely cleansed.

To refresh the aura, rib the bowl around your entire aura, and have a shower of vibrations in your aura.

To cleanse the chakras, place the bowl in front of your first chakra, your base chakra. Connect with your bowl to get the energy flowing easily. Bang the bowl and let it vibrate until you feel it deep inside your first chakra. Repeat for all seven chakras, bowing your head forward in order to connect with your seventh chakra, your crown chakra.

To balance the chakras, simply rib the bowl over all seven chakras. Feel the vibration in each chakra in turn, releasing the stick after each chakra and allowing the vibration to end. Repeat on each chakra as necessary.

When you are giving either yourself or anyone else a full aura and chakra treatment, then there is a sequence to follow. Begin with clearing the aura and then work inwards to cleansing the chakras. Now balance the chakras and work outwards this time to end by balancing or refreshing the aura.

Singing bowls, when played together, create a particular harmony in a wave of harmonic vibrations, and this can bring balance to us on all levels; physical, emotional, mental and Spiritual. These harmonic emissions can relax us, assist in deep meditation, and bring us a deep sense of calm, peace and love, as we listen to their sounds with our heart and not with our ears. We just need to flow with the harmonic vibrations, letting the sound waves resonate with our own frequencies of vibrations to bring us to a state of complete inner balance and peace.

A truly beautiful, balancing, relaxing and re-energising treatment!

CHAPTER 29

ENERGY PROTECTION

Protecting your Energy is of the utmost importance; it is not just optional, but absolutely vital and non-negotiable.

Energy Vampires come in all shapes and forms and situations. They lurk around in the shadows; they strut about in the open, constantly seeking to attack their target, to suck their energy that they so desperately need for their fix. You need to constantly protect your aura and your chakras from these Energy Vampires, and even more so if you are working with healing energies or in any form of holistic therapy. Lower energy forms attract only lower energy forms to them, while higher energy attracts not only higher energies, but also lower energies. In this case, you are a special target for them, and a special trophy when they get you, as your energy is so much higher than the energy of the average person.

These Energy Vampires feed off your energy, giving themselves a boost at your expense. If, at the end of the day, or at any time during the day you feel exhausted, perhaps after talking to someone, for example, or after being in a shopping center, then you have met an Energy Vampire! And they have really feasted on you!

Energy Vampires come in many guises! They can be those who are critical of you, or who try to put you down; those who are jealous of you; make you feel bad about yourself; nag at you; say positive things to your face and then say the opposite about you to others; play on your emotions, the 'poor me' syndrome; claim your attention; demand your time; make you feel guilty, etc.

Other Energy Vampires include radiation; electro-magnetism coming from electrical gadgets, especially computers, mobile phones, televisions, micro-wave ovens, etc, - all electrical equipment which we use every day and to which we are constantly exposed; fertilisers used in gardens; cleaning liquids and abrasives used in household chores; paint; chemical substances.

All of these constantly use up our energy reserves, and we are most often not even aware of it!

None of us can afford to wait until we are attacked; we constantly need protection in order to ward off an imminent attack. We need to maintain a shield around our physical body and our aura, and we need to renew that protection at regular intervals, not just every now and then when we think of it.

And how do we build this shield?

We build and maintain this shield through several methods.

First, we can draw on the White Light, the White Light of the Holy Spirit to surround us on all sides, and around all those whom we wish to protect, as well as places. See yourself, in your mind's eye surrounded by this brilliant White Light and know that you are now protected. Alternatively, you might visualise this radiant White Light hovering above your crown chakra, and then slowly moving down over your entire body, until you are totally enveloped by radiant White Light. This is your protective shield, the White Light of Divine Spirit, impregnable by lower energies or negative forces. You might even see this White Light as a column of light, descending down over your entire body. Or again, you might imagine it as a great white bubble; unzip this huge bubble and step inside, closing up the zip again. You are now safe!

Secondly, you can call on Archangel Michael to cover you with his Blue Cloak; you and all others whom you wish to protect, as well as places. Archangel Michael is the Archangel of protection and strength and never fails to respond to a request.

Thirdly, you can place yourself within the Six-Pointed Star, the Star of the Christ Consciousness, with yourself in the center.

Fourthly, crystals offer protection, especially clear quartz, amethyst, tourmaline, fluoride, etc, and can be easily carried on your person.

Fifthly, organites, which are like crystals, but with copper spirals in their base, which soak up negativity in the atmosphere, are especially effective placed next to computers, micro-wave ovens, televisions, etc. Organites also purify drinking water.

Sixthly, salt lamps which, when lit, purify the air.

In addition, you can cleanse your house, car, etc., with sage, cedar or incense sticks. Cactus plants, all types of crucifix and religious figurines all afford protection.

Symbols too can be used. If, for example, you are attuned to Reiki or any other healing modality, then you can draw or visualise any of those symbols to surround yourself or anyone else with Divine protection.

And of course, prayers, invocations and affirmations are a wonderful source of protection.

Whichever method you choose, you do need to protect yourself at all times. There are lower negative forces and energies all around us as well as the brighter, higher vibrational energies, and we need to keep up our shield, our guard, in order to ensure the lower energies do not get through to lessen or deplete our energy.

Remember! Always maintain your defence mechanism! Always keep up your protective shield!

With your shield, you are always safe!

Temple in Bangkok.

EPILOGUE

A TESTIMONY OF HEALING : MICHELLE'S STORY

My mother was diagnosed with bowel cancer in the Summer of 2015 and was due to have an operation to remove part of her bowel in the late Summer. The week before her final pre-op appointment I opened my calendar for that day and it showed Archangel Raphael, the Archangel of Healing, with the Light emitting from him, and Archangel Raphael's message reminding people to ask for his Healing Light to cover them. My mother is very into Angels and was very open to what I had read. She immediately began to request Archangel Raphael's Healing and continued to do so over the following days.

I was due to attend an Angel and Archangels Workshop in Elysium Wellness in Newry the following Saturday morning with Eileen McCourt. I had read Eileen's first book "Living The Magic" and this was my first experience of joining a Spiritual workshop.

From the very start the energy in the room was palpable due to the combined energies of the other participants, some of them experienced Reiki practitioners and teachers. It was so uplifting to be in a gathering of like-minded people and I immediately felt a great sense of peace and calm in this environment, with a great sense of fun and laughter.

That was the first time I had met Eileen, and I told her after the workshop about my mother and we talked about how I could progress on my Spiritual path. She suggested that I bring my mother in the afternoon to Elysium Wellness for a healing and invited me to remain in the room as well and to observe and get a feel for the energy.

When my mother and I arrived we immediately felt the energy in the room.

Eileen suggested that my hands follow hers around my mother's body in the Reiki hand positions. We called in again the energy of Archangel Raphael and whatever other Celestial Entities would be for my mother's highest good. The heat immediately became very strong in my hands with an intense tingling like pins and needles. Eileen directed me to follow my intuition and place my hands on any particular part to which I was drawn. I immediately felt drawn to my mother's stomach area and kept my hands there while Eileen continued to work around the rest of my mother's body.

The heat in my hands intensified and my mother kept saying that she felt strong heat coming from them into her stomach area. We finished the session after about 45 minutes. My mother was totally exhausted and the tiredness continued for the rest of the evening.

That night she had the best sleep she had had for a long time and felt great the next morning.

Two days later she took a severe pain across her back which left her breathless for about twenty minutes. The next day she was due to attend the hospital for her final pre-op assessment. Before the colonoscopy the doctor told her that her operation would be two days later, but after he had carried out the procedure he informed her that he could find no trace of any cancer and would have to consult his colleagues regarding his findings.

Two weeks later myself and my brother were called to the hospital, with my mother. We were informed by my mother's consultant that following further investigation, no operation would be necessary, as there was no sign of cancer in my mother's bowel.

That was five months ago now and to date there is still no sign of the bowel cancer with which my mother had been previously diagnosed.

My mother and I both have no doubt that this healing was brought about by the healing energy of Archangel Raphael on that Saturday afternoon in Elysium

Wellness in Newry.

I have since completed my Reiki 1 and Reiki 2 with Eileen and also Mother Mary Reiki. I hope to complete my Archangel Reiki Practitioner Course in the New Year.

Michelle McLogan

December 2015

Eileen McCourt